A PRACTICAL GUIDE TO

THE
ORNAMENTAL
GARDEN

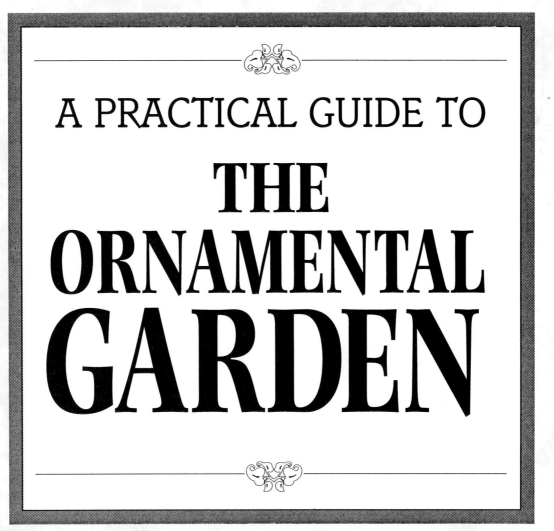

A PRACTICAL GUIDE TO

THE
ORNAMENTAL
GARDEN

‖·PARRAGON·‖

Introduction

Many features can be introduced into a garden and though some, like a children's play area or a summer house to relax in, may only appeal to you at a certain time in your life, others, like ornamental ponds, rock gardens and scree beds, have an appeal throughout your gardening life. Sometimes features can be combined, with the lower part of a rock garden, for example, merging with a pond or scree bed. When creating a new feature in your garden, however, it is important to ensure that it harmonises with others nearby and does not appear to be randomly positioned.

Ideas for new additions to your garden can come from numerous sources. Travelling abroad and looking at gardens often provides inspiration. Though it is not feasible to imitate the 'grand' design of the gardens at Versailles or elaborate, Renaissance-style Italian gardens, it is possible to introduce certain elements from Mediterranean gardens to your own. Oriental gardens, with their clinical but imaginative approach, also have much to offer. Many use water to introduce an element of sparkling freshness to the garden, relying not on a vast area of water but on simple fountains that emerge from a gravel surround. As in many Spanish and Moorish gardens, water is integral to the overall design, creating a cool, refreshing ambience.

Whatever the type of garden, comfortable furniture is essential. Gardening is a cocktail of activity, admiration and relaxation, and unless attractive and comfortable seats and benches are present an entire facet of gardening is lost.

© Marshall Cavendish 1995

Some of this material has previously appeared in the
Marshall Cavendish partwork **My Garden**.

CLB 4381

This edition published 1995 by Parragon Book Services Ltd
Unit 13-17 Avonbridge Trading Estate, Atlantic Road
Avonmouth, Bristol BS11 9QD.

ISBN 1-85813-817-5
Printed in Hong Kong

Contents

An Ornamental Pond

Water brings so many different things to a garden: movement, reflections from the sky, and exciting new plants and wildlife.

A pond is a delightful feature, but is it one that is suitable for every garden? Unfortunately, the answer is no. If a garden is permanently in shade or overshadowed by trees, with little or no open space, then a pond will not be a success. Plants will not thrive and the water will quickly become stagnant.

There are some important aspects to consider before you embark on pond construction. The siting is crucial. It must be open to the sky and not overshadowed by trees. It must also receive sun for a major part of the day.

Water collects at the lowest point of the landscape so bear this in mind: choose the lowest part of the garden, provided it meets with other criteria, especially if you want an informed or 'natural' pond.

Natural landscaping

If you do not have an existing low point try to raise the ground behind the pond so that it appears to be lower than the surrounding ground. For instance, you may be able to create a slope behind it, or construct a rock garden.

Remember also that a pond will create an instant focal point – an object that draws the eye to that part of the garden – so bear this in mind when choosing a site. In formal surroundings a raised pond makes an especially good focal point, especially if it contains a fountain.

Garden style

Assuming your garden has already been designed and laid out, you will need to choose a pond to suit its style.

Basically gardens can be split into two distinct styles. In a formal garden the layout is geometric, based on regular lines and shapes. An informal

Andrew Lawson

Derek Gould

This right-angled pond (above) uses a variety of materials to harmonious effect. The hard edges of bricks and paving slabs are softened by areas of gravel, smooth, round pebbles and plants.

A rockery creates an attractive landscape in an informal garden, echoing the fluid lines of this pond (left). As the dwarf plants already growing on the paving slabs spread further, an even softer effect will be created.

make the plot appear wider than it really is. An L-shaped pond would be suitable for a corner site.

A circular pond might also be suitable in formal surroundings, especially if it has a central fountain. For instance, it could form the centrepiece of a rose garden, or it might be positioned where two paths intersect. This shape would also be suitable for the middle of a lawn.

A half circle would make an excellent focal point at the end of a path or lawn, where it should have a solid background such as a wall or hedge.

A raised pond

If you have a formal garden, you may, of course, prefer a raised pond rather than one on ground level. A raised pond is easily seen so makes an excellent focal point.

A raised pond is certainly highly recommended for two formal areas not so far mentioned: the patio and the courtyard garden. Indeed, a raised pond is the norm in a classic courtyard and often features a fountain. The walls of the pond, which may be square, rectangular or circular, can be

Andrew Lawson

SAFETY FIRST

DON'T FORGET!

A pond can be a great danger to small children. If you start off with a sunken sandpit for toddlers, when they are older it can easily be converted into a pond. Simply line the hole with a rubber or PVC pond liner or instal a preformed pond unit.

A simple, plain, rectangular shape (above) is the perfect choice in this formal paved garden.

Even with only a tiny corner, you can still have a pond. Make sure you have a clear idea of the style, though. This pond (below) would have been a better design with either straight, paved sides or a curved stone edge.

garden has no straight lines. Of course, these are very basic guidelines; there are lots of variations on each style.

Formal gardens

For a garden with beds and borders of regular shapes and straight paths, you should choose a square or rectangular pond. A square pond often makes a good feature in the centre of a formal layout. A rectangular pond positioned across a narrow garden will

Derek Gould

Peter McHoy

Ron Sutherland/Garden Picture Library

This uncluttered patio pool has a cunningly hidden water source feeding into the pond through an overturned urn (above), creating a stylish, modern effect. Another unusual water source (below) is this lion's head. It creates an exciting corner in a walled garden. Note, too, the stunning contrast of scarlet geraniums against whitewashed walls.

capped with coping stones. These give a neat finish and can be used as additional seating.

On a patio, or indeed in any other area of the garden, there is no need to stick to just one raised pond. Why not have several interlocking ponds on different levels? For instance, consider a group of several small square ponds, with a submerged pump to circulate water so that it cascades from one to another.

An informal style

Informal gardens have beds, borders and lawns of irregular shape, with smooth 'flowing' edges and no squared-off corners. The pond should be of similar style.

The shape is up to you, but bear in mind that an informal pond only looks right at ground level or below. One suggestion would be to have a longish pond which is broad at one end, ideal for displaying water lilies, and then gradually tapers to the other end until it becomes quite narrow, making an ideal home for tall aquatic plants.

A natural pond to attract wild creatures would be a good choice for a garden that has areas of long grass and wild flowers. The natural pond should be slightly sunken, with grass right down to the water's edge, to enable any wildlife to reach the water easily.

Practical points

These days ponds are comparatively simple to construct using modern flexible liners or preformed units. These need little or no maintenance if installed correctly.

The pros and cons of ground-level and raised ponds may well influence your choice. The main advantage of a ground-level pond is that you will have lots of soil left over for creating another feature such as a rock garden. It will also work out cheaper. A major disadvantage is that it can be hard work digging out the soil. You may not actually want the soil and will then have the problem of disposing of it.

A raised pond does not have to be excavated and can be built on any site. The building materials are expensive, however. If using bricks or

Neil Holmes

This unusual formal pond (right) is in an enclosed courtyard. It not only creates an agreeable background to al fresco eating, it gives the unusual impression that the patio is actually floating on the water! Note that care has been taken to site the pond in an area of the garden which is not overshadowed by trees.

This informal pond surrounded by rocks and gravel (left) has a perfect open aspect for its plants to thrive in the sun. The choice of ornaments and plants combine to give the pool a Japanese feel.

Neil Holmes

This tiny, sunken pond (below) is stocked full of plants and fish and creates a delightfully cooling and informal effect in this very sunny garden.

ornamental concrete walling blocks you have to be quite skilled at bricklaying and, invariably, it will take a little more time to construct.

You will be more restricted as regards size and shape if you opt for a preformed pond unit, although formal and informal designs are available. Make sure you buy a unit that is deep enough, as some preformed ponds are not of the minimum 45cm/18in depth and should be avoided.

The major advantage of a preformed unit is that it enables you to make a pond quickly and easily. Generally it is fitted into a square or rectangular hole with sand in the bottom and packed firmly around with more sand. Always follow the suppliers'

MATERIALS AVAILABLE

- **Black butyl rubber** is the most expensive type of flexible liner, has the longest life, is less prone to damage and is repairable.

- **PVC liners** are cheaper and of variable quality. A reinforced laminated layer is strongest and will last longest. The best colours are black or stone.

- **Polyester matting** is used to line a pond excavation, as well as sand, if the ground is very stony, prior to installing a flexible liner.

- **Preformed glass fibre** units are strong and have a long life.

- **Preformed plastic** units are cheaper but are still quite strong. They do not last as long as glass fibre. Black is the best colour.

GARDEN NOTES

Andrew Lawson

INFORMAL PLANTING

Use these plants for effective planting in informal and natural ponds

● double marsh marigold (*Caltha palustris* 'Plena') has golden-yellow flowers

● iris (*Iris laevigata*) varieties have sword-shaped leaves

● bog bean *(Menyanthes trifoliata)* has white fringed flowers

● forget-me-not (*Myosotis palustris*) has tiny blue flowers

● greater spearwort (*Ranunculus lingua* 'Grandiflorus') has buttercup-like flowers

● yellow water or pond lily (*Nuphar lutea*) has yellow flowers. It is vigorous and only for large ponds

● soft rush (*Juncus effusus*) has thick green stems

● water mint (*Mentha aquatica)* has aromatic foliage and lilac-pink flowers

● reed mace (*Typha angustifolia*) has brown, sausage-like flower spikes

instructions on installation in case there are any special requirements.

A flexible liner enables you to construct a pond of any shape or size. To calculate the size you need, multiply the overall length of pond required by twice the depth. This will give you the length of liner you need. To find its width, multiply the overall width of pond by twice its depth. For an informal shape, make the calculation by using the greatest width and length. The usual depth for a garden pond is 45-60cm/18-24in.

When you have made the

Once an informal pond is well established, the plants in and around it merge to create a wonderfully romantic effect. This pool (top left) is overhung with peonies and variegated shrubs and filled with water lilies and the sunny, buttercup-like flowers of Ranunculus lingua 'Grandiflorus'.

The golden-yellow flowers of the double marsh marigold, Caltha palustris 'Plena', (above left), are some of the first to bloom in the water garden. They grow best in shallow water on boggy soil at the side of a natural pond.

hole for the pond, drap the liner loosely inside it and secure with bricks around the edge, leaving an overlap. Fill with water and gradually ease off the bricks as the liner stretches. Edge the pond with concrete or stone slabs, to hide the overlap.

Pond plants

Water lilies and marginal aquatics (those grown in the shallow water around the edge of a pond) can be planted in most ponds, although the quantity and types used should be determined by the style of your pond.

Water marginals, such as flags merge with water lilies in this sunken pond (right) to great effect. Creating a shallow ledge when you build your pond, means you can cultivate a much greater selection of plants and you can also disguise the edge of your pond.

This natural pond (left) merges beautifully into its surroundings. It has an excellent colour balance with its purple iris (I. laevigata 'Variegata') set against the yellow flag iris (I. pseudacorus).

Water in the garden has many functions. It can, for instance, be used not so much as a feature in its own right but as an integral part of a natural environment (below) which will attract wildlife to your garden.

Eric Crichton

Photos Horticultural

As the water itself is often the main feature of a formal pond, few plants are generally used, but it is up to you to decide what will suit your garden. The surface may be punctuated by a group or two of water lilies, for example, and the edges planted with a few clumps of distinctive bold 'architectural' aquatics. Look at the plant list (far right) for ideas and inspiration.

An informal pond, on the other hand, can be densely planted. Use plenty of water lilies and less formal-looking marginals such as marsh marigolds or flags.

PLANTS FOR FORMAL PONDS

- sweet flag (*Acorus calamus* 'Variegatus') has sword-shaped leaves striped with cream and green

- variegated water grass (*Glyceria aquatica* 'Variegata') has grassy green and cream stripped leaves

- variegated yellow flag (*Iris pseudacorus* 'Variegata') has sword-shaped leaves striped with cream and green

- pickerel weed (*Pontederia cordata*) has lance-shaped leaves and blue flowers

- zebra rush (*Scirpus tabernaemontani* 'Zebrinus') has stems barred white and green

- bog arum (*Calla palustris*) has white, sail-like flowers and heart-shaped leaves

- double Japanese arrowhead (*Sagittaria sagittifolia* 'Flore Pleno') has arrow-shaped leaves and white double flowers

- white water lily (*Nymphaea alba*) has white flowers with yellow stamens

A Water Garden

A water feature enhances any garden, and provides a home for a host of attractive plants, both in the water and around its edges.

Water is an important element in garden design, beautiful in itself. The tinkle of running water, whether it plays from a fountain or falls from a ledge, has a soothing, relaxing effect, while a still pool reflects the colours and moods of the sky and clouds and sends shafts of sunlight dancing across the garden.

Water is also a growing medium for plants. Whether you have a formal pool complete with fountain, a small stream, or a sprawling, naturalistic pond, the right choice of plants can enhance its beauty. Even a stubbornly soggy patch in a forgotten corner of the garden can be made a feature.

Wild life

A well-planted water garden also makes an attractive environment for a host of interesting and colourful insects, amphibians and fish.

Brightly-coloured damsel flies and dragonflies hover and flutter across the surface and cling to the leaves, while pond-skaters dart across the limpid water.

Frogs, toads and newts will quickly colonize a pond, producing masses of spawn in the spring and helping to keep the slug population down.

Fish will, of course, have to be introduced, unless you are lucky enough to have a stream flowing through the garden. Goldfish will feed on spawn and tadpoles, but so will native fish, and even cats! There is no need to exclude them on wildlife grounds, and their darting, sun-gold presence near the surface in warm weather is always a boon.

Birds also enjoy visiting ponds, both for drinking and bathing. They need shallow water for this, so make sure there is a ledge or a gentle slope at at least one place in the pond that they can use. Frogs, toads and newts also require this sort of access point if they are to get in and out of the water easily.

Plants naturally increase the wild life potential of a water feature; their flowers attract insects while their leaves and stems make perches for them, as well as offering shade and shelter at the water's edge for birds and amphibians.

Some plants perform special

Even a small pool can be home to a number of attractive flowering and foliage plants (above). Here, a small, non-classical statue provides a focus in a basically informal design incorporating lilies and several marginal plants.

BE PATIENT

In its first season your pond will look a bit sparsely planted. Don't be tempted to overplant as the majority of water plants usually spread quickly and will need cutting back and dividing in a season or two.

Marginals can be planted according to the same principles as a bed (right). A variegated grass gives height and water mint (Mentha aquatica) dark, aromatic leaves. A monkey flower (Mimulus luteus) provides yellow flowers, and water forget-me-not (Myosotis scorpioides), blue ones.

Pat Brindley

Andrew Lawson

There are many ways of bringing a small pond to life with summer colour. One traditional solution is to plant one or two varieties from the enormous water lily genus; Nymphaea 'Froebelii' (right) adds to the appeal of its flowers with mottled leaves. The appeal of water lilies is enhanced by stocking your pond with ornamental fish. Goldfish or koi carp (above) swim close to the surface on warm days, flashing gold and silver in the sunshine, and, providing the pond is not too shallow, can survive weeks of icy weather in the winter.

Tania Midgley

tasks, cleaning and oxygenating the water to improve the environment, or preventing the build up of algae, the primitive, microscopic plants that discolour the water, and make a green slick over pebbles and other surfaces.

The ripple effect

There are plants to suit all watery environments: deep or shallow water; pond margins, swamp or wet land.

You can create a succession of bands of plants, according to the amount of moisture they like around their roots. These bands move out from the deep centre of the pond like the ripples made by a stone thrown into a pool. Each ripple performs an important function, as well as providing colour and ornament to the design.

Plants that live in the centre of the pond are known as deep-water aquatics. They root at the bottom of the pond, either in planting crates or in a layer of soil, while their leaves and flowers float at, or just above, the surface.

The best-known deep-water aquatics are the water lilies (*Nymphaea spp.*). Hybridiz-

PLANTING TIMES

Plant water gardens in spring and early summer. Warmer water, rising air temperatures and longer hours of daylight all encourage strong growth.

If you've just filled a pool with water, let it stand for up to ten days to allow the chlorine in tap water to evaporate.

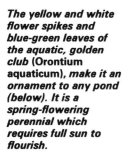

The yellow and white flower spikes and blue-green leaves of the aquatic, golden club (Orontium aquaticum), *make it an ornament to any pond (below). It is a spring-flowering perennial which requires full sun to flourish.*

Photos Horticultural

Jean Hall/Nature Photographers

ation has created a range of varieties to suit anyone's taste or the size of their pond.

Excellent alternatives include the water hawthorn (*Aponogeton distachyus*) whose small white flowers have a scent like hawthorn blossom, and the golden club (*Orontium aquaticum*), which produces long, yellow and white flower spikes.

Most of these plants have large, flat leaves that are attractive in themselves but also provide good shade, preventing the growth of algae.

The breath of life
Every still pond needs oxygenating plants if it is to support a wide variety of life. Like deep-water aquatics, oxygenating plants have their roots and stems submerged. The difference is that their leaves are under water, too.

This means that they aerate the water, keeping it clear. All plants produce oxygen as a by-product of converting sunlight into food and respire it through their leaves; oxygen-

Among the most attractive marginal plants is the flowering rush (Butomus umbellatus). *Its twisting green leaves give height at the side of a pond, but it is grown mainly for its heads of pink and red summer flowers (above).*

PLANTING

It's best to plant aquatics and marginals in plastic baskets with perforated sides. They can then be removed from the pond in autumn when you want to thin them or remove dead foliage, and it is easier to handle any plants that may become diseased.

Marginals can be planted in the soil at the water's edge, but they are easier to handle – and much easier to lift for thinning out or division – if they are planted in perforated plastic baskets specially designed for the purpose (right).

ating plants release it directly into the water, rather than into the atmosphere.

This is a bonus for fish, which breathe the oxygen, although in shaded or overcast conditions the oxygen is produced at a much slower rate.

The underwater foliage provides shelter, nutrients and breeding grounds for fish and newts. It also has a vital preventative function. The leaves absorb mineral nutrients from the water, depriving algae of vital foods.

Many oxygenating plants are decorative as well as useful. The water starwort (*Callitriche verna* syn *C. palustris*) has feathery, divided leaves

Andrew Lawson

Most water lilies require room to spread. The sweetly-scented Nymphaea 'Odorata Alba' (above) is an exception, however, flourishing in relatively small pools.

that swirl into attractive shapes just below the surface, and carries its delicate flowers high above the water, while water milfoil (*Myriophyllum spicatum*) has red-tipped, feathery foliage.

Be sure to avoid invasive oxygenating plants such as Canadian pondweed (*Elodea canadensis*). Goldfish weed (*Elodea crispa*) is an attractive, non-rampant alternative.

Floating plants

Many water plants do not need to root in soil at all. Instead, they float across the pond, pushed by winds and the movement of water wildlife.

Fairy moss (*Azolla caroliniana*) is a tiny plant that spreads quickly to form a dense mat. In spring, it is coloured a fresh green: in autumn it turns russet-red. It tends to be invasive, but it is easy enough to control in a small pond, as you can simply

Pat Brindley

Those lucky enough to have a stream running through, or at the end of, their garden, will find that they can clothe its banks with the many colourful garden plants that appreciate moist soil (left). Here, the flower-heads of various species of achillea combine with rock roses (Helianthemum spp.), monkey flowers (Mimulus spp.), the mat-forming speedwell (Veronica prostrata) and others to make a wonderful summer display.

ON STREAM

If you have a stream or a ditch and bank at the end of the garden, plant it with native wild flowers that enjoy moist conditions. Ferns such as marsh buckler (*Thelypteris palustris*) will do well on the shady banks.

At the water's edge, tuck in marsh marigold. Ragged robin (*Lychnis flos-cuculi*), with its feathery, rose-coloured flowers, will naturalize quickly in sunnier spots along the bank.

The cheery yellow flowers of the flag (Iris pseudacorus), *held aloft on stems as much as 1.5m/5ft tall – though usually a little less – brighten up a pondside. The yellow leaf stripes of 'Variegata' (left) fade after the plant flowers in early to mid summer.*

David Squire

Brian Carter/Garden Picture Library

FERTILIZERS

Special aquatic fertilizer with a high phosphate content is available. It is slowly released throughout the growing season. Don't use ordinary fertilizer or manure as these rapidly dissolve and will boost algal growth.

IMPROVING A BOG

If your bog garden is on a clay or heavy soil that holds water too well in winter and loses it spectacularly in summer, when it bakes to a brick-hard consistency, your moisture-loving bog garden plants will die.

To lighten and improve the drainage, work in well-rotted organic matter and mulch around the plant roots after watering it thoroughly.

If the soil is light and sandy, create a boggy patch by digging an area near the pond, covering it with a piece of pond-liner and filling with organic matter and soil. Flood it when you top up the pond, and you will be able to plant it up with moisture-loving plants.

lift out any excessive growth with a fine-meshed net.

Like deep-water aquatics, floating plants are excellent at controlling algae. The floating mats of leaves move across the water, soaking up the sunlight the algae need.

Marginals

Marginal plants such as rushes and flags (yellow water irises) grow at the edges of ponds. They like to have their roots in shallow water – from 5-30cm/2-12in – or, like the dwarf Japanese rush (*Acorus gramineus* 'Variegatus'), at water level.

When marginal plants are well-established they soften the edges of a pond, hiding plastic liners or other obtrusive, structural features. They also provide shelter for emerging froglets and for birds.

Otherwise, marginals are purely decorative. Most of them have an upright habit, providing a strong vertical emphasis against the horizontal surface of the pond. Many also have fine flowers, such as the marsh marigold (*Caltha palustris*), which produces a brilliant profusion of yellow flowers in spring, the flowering rush (*Butomus umbellatus*), whose small rose-pink flowers wave from tall, elegant stems, and the yellow flag (*Iris pseudacorus*).

Some plants enjoy growing

You do not need a lot of space or a sprawling informal pond to house a good selection of water plants (above). In this patio, a pond has been created by building up the sides rather than digging, and a raised central area allows for the planting of aquatics that require different depths of water in which to flourish.

Andrew Lawson

A bog area makes a good home for many moisture-loving decorative plants (above). Here, the grassy foliage of a sedge and the spreading leaves of a hosta provide the background for the feathery pink flowers of astilbe.

The mimulus genus has produced a number of modern hybrid varieties, much showier than the species, with the yellow flowers heavily speckled with red. Many can flourish in a border, but all look best at the margins of a pond (below).

in the permanently soggy conditions around the edges of an informal pool, and can be used to bridge the gap between the pond and the planting in rest of the garden.

This is particulary true of those such as *Astilbe* spp., bugle (*Ajuga reptans*) and plantain lilies (*Hosta* spp.), all of which also grow happily in other parts of the garden.

Some waterside plants are tall-growing or large-leaved and will provide dramatic focal points. If you have the space, giant rhubarb (*Gunnera manicata*) gives you a mound of huge, spreading rhubarb-type leaves and a tall central flower spike.

Finishing touch

To complete the ripple effect of your water garden planting, add a tree or two. Many trees grow naturally in wet conditions, and will make a graceful backdrop to a wild-life water garden or at the top of a bank.

Willow and birch are full of year-round interest, with attractive bark and outlines in winter, catkins in spring, and foliage in summer and autumn. Do not plant trees too close, however; they cast shade and fallen leaves will pollute the water.

David Squire

Stocking a Pond

Although not essential to creating a natural balance, fish and other aquatic creatures add life to a pond and give it the appearance of being a natural rather than a man-made garden feature.

Watching fish is a soothing pastime for adults, and youngsters find pond life fascinating. Your pond will provide a valuable habitat for many wild creatures that spend all or part of their time in water.

Pond life can be beneficial in other ways, too. Fish will eat several unpleasant pond pests, such as mosquito larvae. These are the small squiggly creatures found just under the surface of the water in summer. Adult mosquitoes visit the pond to breed, but linger in gardens and cause nasty bites. Fish also take water plant pests such as aphids and water lily beetles.

Fish excreta provides a natural fertilizer for water plants. And the carbon dioxide fish exhale when they breathe is used by submerged plants in photosynthesis.

Frogs, toads and newts visit the water to breed. The adults benefit gardeners by feeding on slugs, snails and beetles in the garden.

Water snails help the pond, keeping the water clean by feeding on algae, while freshwater mussels act as living water filters.

Buying fish

Fish can be bought from water garden departments of garden centres, fish farms or, by post, from mail order water garden specialists. (See ads in gardening magazines).

Where possible, choose your own fish so you can be sure of getting healthy specimens. Healthy fish move quickly and have a good colour. Avoid sluggish fish or those with disease spots and obvious injuries.

Do not buy more fish than your pond can support. As a rough guide allow one square metre of pond surface to each 15cm of fish (about 11 square feet for a 6-inch fish). Stock the pond first at a quarter this rate, to allow for the fish growing.

The ultimate size that fish will reach is determined by the size of the pond and the amount of oxygen in the water.

Adding a fountain or waterfall helps oxygenate the pond, especially in warm weather when the water holds a great deal less oxygen.

When stocking the pond, select fish of roughly the same size, otherwise large fish may bully the smaller ones.

Types of fish

Goldfish, shubunkin and golden orfe are probably the best choice for a small garden pond. These are all colourful fish which show up well, and swim close to the surface where they

Beautiful golden-orange fish and a wide variety of water and marginal plants (above) all help to make this pond a peaceful retreat from the stresses and strains of modern life.

Peter McHoy

A relative of the goldfish, the shubunkin (left) is a popular choice of fish for a garden pond. Easy to care for, its bright colours and habit of swimming close to the surface give it considerable ornamental appeal.

The freshwater winkle (below) is a valuable addition to a pond because it helps to control the spread of algae by scraping it off underwater stones and plants.

BREEDING FISH

Goldfish and shubunkins readily breed in garden ponds. The eggs hatch out to produce hundreds of minute transparent 'fry'. Unfortunately, both these and fish eggs are eaten – often by the parents themselves – so very few live to become adults.

If you want fish to breed successfully, it is essential to provide plenty of water weeds in which the fry can take cover.

can be seen and admired.

Avoid catfish and tench, which are bottom feeders and stir up the mud, making the water murky. Catfish are also aggressive; they bully other fish and, unfortunately, can often cause serious injuries.

Koi carp need a large pond which should be 1-1.2m/3-4ft deep, ideally with moving water. Where possible, install a pump with an external filter through which the water is pumped, perhaps feeding a waterfall.

Koi live mainly at the bottom of the pond, where they root around, stirring up mud and dislodging water plants. So take extra care to bed oxygenating plants under a heavy rock and use large planting baskets for water lilies.

G.I. Bernard/NHPA

Introducing fish

Do not be in too much of a hurry to add fish after making your pond. If the pond is concrete, change the water a couple of times over the next two weeks or buy a product from your pond supplier that neutralizes the lime in the concrete immediately. Modern butyl, plastic or glass fibre liners can be filled and planted as soon as they are put in. But allow about a week for the water to warm up and any chlorine to disappear before adding fish.

With established ponds, most people think about adding fish in spring. But you can do so in summer, if the kinds you want are available.

Fish are normally supplied in large polythene bags which have been inflated and tied at the neck. This prevents water

GROWING TIPS

FEEDING FISH

Various types of pond fish foods are available. The flaked type is most suitable for young fish, as it breaks up into tiny fragments that even the smallest fish can swallow. Floating pellets are often used for larger fish, particularly koi, which can otherwise be difficult to persuade up to the surface.

Feed fish daily from mid spring to late autumn, giving them as much as they can finish within ten minutes. High protein foods, such as daphnia and tubifex worms (normally bought dry but sometimes live), are recommended for feeding in spring and autumn, when fish need building up either side of their winter rest.

If you always feed fish at the same time and the same place, they will come to associate you with food and may eat out of your hand. Koi carp, particularly, are easy to 'tame'. During winter, fish scarcely feed and any food in the water may go bad.

The ever popular goldfish (below) will thrive even in the smallest pond.

Harry Smith Collection

FISH AND OTHER WILDLIFE FOR A POND

Goldfish Chunky orange fish, many variants available with bulging eyes, long flowing fins and tails, etc; of these only long-tailed comets are really suitable outdoors.

Shubunkin Colourful goldfish relative, with blue, purple, red or orange markings on a lighter body. Strong colours most sought after.

Golden orfe Slim, pencil-shaped orange fish that swims in shoals and darts about close to the surface. Can reach 38cm/15in in a large pond. Rarely breeds in temperate ponds.

Koi carp Spectacularly coloured fish in a variety of colours and patterns (koi enthusiasts have Japanese names to describe fish with particular markings). Long-lived fish, easily tamed to feed from the hand; can grow very big in a large pond.

Common frog Adult: smooth moist skin, moves by hopping; breeds from late winter to mid spring. Spawn: large jelly-like masses floating near surface of water; it hatches in a few weeks. Tadpoles: black or dark brown tadpoles, rounded tips to tails, swimming in shallow water near pond edge.

Common toad Adult: rough, dry, warty skin, walks rather than hops. Breeds in mid spring. Spawn: long double strands which sink to the bottom of the pond and tangle in water weeds; hatches in a few weeks. Tadpoles: dark brown, tails have pointed tips and goldish speckles.

Newts Several species, like lizards but with broad, paddle-like tails. Breed in mid spring. Eggs: individual, stuck to underside of water plants. Tadpoles: big feathery gills protrude from sides of head. Slow to mature, they don't become young newts until early autumn.

Freshwater whelk Whelk-shaped, feeds on submerged water plants; inadvisable.

Ramshorn snails Shells shaped like Catherine wheels, black or reddish; beneficial.

Freshwater winkle Winkle-like snail; beneficial.

Dragonflies Large, vividly coloured insects that dart over ponds; lay eggs on water plants. These hatch into ferocious larvae that feed on water insects etc; take a year to develop.

Water boatman and pond skaters Fast-moving insects that shoot back and forth across the water on warm days. Pond skaters are harmless but water boatmen may attack small fish.

slopping about in the car, and ensures the fish are safe.

When you get them home, float the bag, still tied at the neck, in the pond. This allows the fish to acclimatize to the temperature of the water. After at least an hour, untie the neck of the bag and allow it to slowly fill with water.

Make sure the neck is wide open, so that the fish can swim out when they are ready. Avoid tipping or handling them, as they are easily damaged, and injured fish usually die.

Amphibians

Amphibious animals – frogs, toads and newts – are delightful to have in and around a pond. Adults return to the pond they hatched out in to breed, if necessary crossing miles of inhospitable countryside to do so.

A good way to ensure a crop of tadpoles each year is to introduce spawn in the first place. These can sometimes be obtained from friends, through wildlife trusts or from schools. Young tadpoles are preyed on by fish, so provide plenty of pondweed to give them somewhere to hide.

By midsummer, when tadpoles are growing their front legs, they will need to get out of the water occasionally. Give them a large stone as an 'island', or provide a ramp if the pond does not have any

Stephen Dalton/NHPA

The tiny water boatman (above right) can sometimes be seen skimming across the water on warm, summer days. Unfortunately, it can attack small fish and pond owners should keep an eye out for it.

Frogs are one of the most delightful amphibians to encourage in and around ponds (right). Often they will appear of their own accord; otherwise, introduce frog spawn, obtainable through wildlife trusts or from schools.

Ron Sutherland/Garden Picture Library

gently shelving sides.

Water snails are valuable in ponds as they help to control some algae.

Molluscs

The best kind are ramshorn snails (which have shells shaped like Catherine wheels). Freshwater winkles are also useful. Both feed by scraping algae from underwater stones and plants.

The snail often sold for ponds, however, is the freshwater whelk. These feed on water plants, especially the oxygenators, so should not be introduced. They can be caught by floating a cabbage or lettuce leaf on the water, and removing the snails that gather under it daily.

All water snails are hermaphrodites and breed fast. Their eggs and young are readily snapped up by fish.

The other useful pond mollusc is the swan mussel, which lives by filtering water through its large shell. This helps to keep the water clear. Swan mussels grow 10-13cm/ 4-5in long. They are rarely seen, as they lie on the floor of the pond and hardly move, though they can shuffle about.

When feeding, the mussel extends a whitish tube through the slightly open shell and sucks water through it. Like snails, the mussel's young form part of the diet of fish. Enough young survive to replace the parents.

Eric Crichton

The pond habitat

A well set up pond should provide shade, protection from predators and food. For shade, grow water lilies and floating plants such as azolla, plus clumps of tall marginal plants round the edge – water irises, lythrum, primulas, arrowhead and others.

Predators of pond life include herons, hedgehogs, foxes and domestic cats. Herons visit early in the morning. An artificial heron standing close to the pond may deter them, but is not always successful.

Since herons wade into the pond rather than flying into it, they can be put off by stretching a nylon line (such as thick fishing line) 10-15cm/4-6in high round the pond edge.

A line may also help deter hedgehogs, foxes and cats. If these are a regular nuisance, it may be worth trying several lines at various heights. But in really bad cases, cover the pond with a net that is well secured round the edge.

Mosquito larvae, water fleas (daphnia) and other insects, including flies, which settle on the water will all be taken by fish, tadpoles and adult amphibians. So, too, will the jelly-like egg masses of water snails, which are laid on the under surface of lily leaves and on weeds.

Given a large enough pond, there will be enough natural food. But in small ornamental ponds a certain amount of extra feeding is necessary (see box on page 1097).

Spectacular ornamental koi carp (above) need a large, deep pond with moving water in order to flourish. With patience, some of them can become tame enough to eat out of your hand.

Canadian pondweed (below) helps keep pond water oxygenated. In winter, when other plants have died down, it gives protection to fish; in summer, it provides deep shade.

ESSENTIAL OXYGENATOR

Canadian pondweed (*Elodea canadensis*) should be in every pond stocked with fish. It is an evergreen oxygenating plant, so it keeps on working, even in winter when other oxygenators have died down.

Besides giving off vital oxygen all year round, it provides valuable cover for fish, giving them somewhere to hide from herons and other predators in winter. In summer, it provides deep shade where fish can escape from the sun, and allows tiny fish fry to hide from larger fish.

Buy it in unrooted bunches. Anchor three clumps to stones or plant in proper planting baskets, and sink close together in the middle of the pond.

GO ORGANIC!

Stephen Dalton/NHPA

Fountains and Cascades

Moving water is a garden feature in its own right. Fountains, cascades and streams will add musical notes and shimmering accents to even a small garden.

The sound of water splashing, tinkling or sighing over rocks brings a magical element to your garden. Sunlight playing on a fountain fills the air with a sparkling array of jewel-like droplets. The sight and sound of moving water brings tranquillity and grace to a world that is all too often short of both.

While ponds are an accepted feature in many small gardens, moving water features are not so familiar. If you are planning to introduce moving water into your garden, it is a useful plan to find out what is available to buy before you do anything else.

This is a specialized area of gardening, and it pays to consult specialists. If possible, visit a water garden centre to gain inspiration and to collect catalogues. It is a good idea to leave your cheque book and credit card at home for this initial visit, as it is all too easy to get carried away! If there is no suitable centre in your area, send for a selection of mail order catalogues for inspiration and price comparisons.

Pump power

Unless you have a talent for engineering and a garden that boasts a spring or a natural gradient, you are going to need a pump to move water from one place to another.

It is important to choose the right pump for the job. Commercially available ones tend to vary in power from 50 watts to 175 watts. Each pump can be set to move a large volume of water a short way or jet a smaller volume over a larger distance. A 50 watt pump, for

Eric Crichton

example, will shift 400 gallons per hour about 15cm/6in or 50 g.p.h. 1.5m/5ft.

There are two types of pump; one is submerged in your pond while the other is sited on dry land nearby. Surface or external types tend to use less power than submersible pumps and are therefore cheaper to run. They are also more accessible for maintenance, as you do not have to drag them out of the pond.

On the debit side, surface pumps must be housed in a waterproof, well-ventilated chamber because, surprising-

Fountains freshen the air as well as delighting the eye and ear. One or two of them can lend enchantment to a small pond for relatively little outlay. Here, a tiny lily pool is transformed by three cherubs.

JET SET

You might think that once you have opted for a fountain, chosen your design and selected the right pump, all that is left is the installation. However, there is one more decision to make; you have to choose the kind of spray you would like.

Scale is important. If the jet is too vigorous, it could overpower the pond and the whole design, making it look ridiculous. If it is too feeble, it may look insignificant.

Different jet nozzles produce a range of wonderful effects. Bubble jets are the ones to choose for millstone or pebble features, and work well feeding small cascades and streams.

There are jets that make handsome bell and dome shapes. More delicate effects are achieved by using stepped jets, which produce slender sprays of water at varying heights. Fancier still are stepped jets that make the water twist and turn in pirouettes.

Some jets combine a bell shape with a central spray, while others produce an eruption of foaming water like a small volcano. Inverted cones, circles and hemispheres are also possible.

Harry Smith Collection

ly, they are easily damaged by moisture getting into the wrong places. You must also be vigilant and ensure that the pump is always primed, or its motor will burn out.

Submersible pumps tend to be less powerful, but this will not be a problem unless you are planning a large, impressive water feature. They are adequate for most purposes and have several advantages.

Silent and invisible, they are relatively easy to clean, although you do have to fish them out of your pond to do it. Best of all, they need no priming, so there is less risk of burning the motor out.

Glazed pottery is an unusual material for a fountain, but its colour and sheen make it eminently suitable (right above). In this two-tiered example, water is pumped from the lower basin to the upper one.

Terracotta lends itself to every style, from rustic to classical (right). This fountain is also self-contained; the dish of pebbles into which the urn pours is part of the design.

The sound of moving water can easily be introduced into the severest of formal designs (below).

Harry Smith Collection

Harry Smith Collection

It is better to decide on what effect you want and then to choose the pump that will achieve it. Do not buy the pump first and then try to work out what it will do. The equation is tricky, so it is best to seek expert advice. Catalogues give clear tables and staff at water garden centres are experienced in such matters and are there to help you.

Which feature?

It is important to consider several factors carefully before committing yourself. Firstly, do you intend to have a moving

23

Derek Gould

There are many designs available in kit form that require no plumbing in. All they need is electricity to run the pump.

Safety is another important issue, especially if you have young children. Once again, a freestanding fountain is the answer, bringing the sound of moving water to your garden with no risk of anyone drowning. Millstone or pebble fountains are particularly good under these circumstances. Just make sure that the wiring that powers them is out of the way of small fingers.

Self-contained fountains are useful in a small space. They may be placed on patios, in borders or under trees. It is also possible to have a unit attached to a wall, if ground space is at a premium.

A question of style

The next thing to think about is what sort of feature will look best in your garden.

Fountains fall loosely into four main styles; classical, traditional, oriental and informal. Graceful, classical fountain designs usually take the form of figures clad in flowing robes. Often, they pour water from urns, jugs or shells into the pool or into a single or tiered basin. These designs look stunning as the centre piece of a formal design, but

A slightly larger fountain provides a valuable vertical accent, and brightens up a shady corner (above). This design is typical of the traditional style, which often features boys or cherubs with various water creatures such as fishes, dolphins and frogs.

A stylized fish – often referred to as a dolphin – is another typical traditional design. Here (right) it is married to a more modern idea, a brick-built basin filled with pebbles.

Harry Smith Collection

water feature as part of a pool or pond, or will it stand alone?

Ponds with plants require a site in full sun. If this is not feasible in your garden, then a freestanding, self-contained fountain is your best bet.

LIGHT ON THE WATER

There is a range of lighting units that will enable you to enjoy your water feature at night.

A floodlight or lamp situated outside the pond can highlight the spray. Coloured filters give you a choice of green, amber, red and blue light. A revolving filter will allow a succession of colours to play over the fountain.

Submersible units are excellent for this purpose; underlighting adds to the drama of a fountain. Once again, colour can be controlled by the filter you choose. Some fountains include a light as an integral part of their design.

Tania Midgley

would be absurdly out of place in a wildlife pond.

Traditional designs are usually less imposing. Cherubs, dolphins and elegantly shaped plants like tulips or lilies feature large here. Once again, self-contained kits are readily available.

Oriental designs make lovely features in Japanese gardens. The choice includes lanterns, dragons and pagodas as well as the traditional simplicity of the *shishi odoshi*, a bamboo construction that was originally used as an ingenious bird and animal scarer to protect crops and gardens. A gentle stream of water gradually fills a balanced bamboo pipe that eventually tips up, giving a strategically placed rock a solid knock as it empties, and returning to its original position to be refilled.

If you have an informal or cottage garden and would like to include a fountain, a millstone or pebble feature, with water bubbling gently up from the centre and trickling out to the edges, is perhaps the best choice. These have a rustic air that blends in well with infor-

mal surroundings. Other informal designs include all manner of birds and beasts and, of course, garden gnomes.

As an alternative to fountains, waterfalls, streams and cascades mimic the natural world and therefore lend themselves to an informal setting. A wildlife garden will not stand the artificiality of a

fountain but may be enhanced with a spring, a babbling brook or a waterfall. These features will aerate the pond water and prove a delight to the gardener and pond-dwellers alike.

Kits for cascades, waterfalls and streams, including liners and pumps, are widely available and simple to install. An-

A naturalistic waterfall (above) brings the music of moving water into an informal setting.

Another simple, but effective alternative is to have water pouring from a pipe set into a brick retaining wall (below) to give the impression of an emergent spring.

Eric Crichton

own water. Maintenance is also simple, as long as you follow the manufacturer's instructions carefully.

Materials

Materials vary; your choice will depend on what you want and how much you can afford. Reconstructed stone is the most expensive option, but it does have the advantage of acquiring a patina of mosses and lichens in time, thus giving the impression of age. Most fountains are made of this hard-wearing material and are guaranteed frost-proof.

Concrete fountains and statues are cheaper than stone but do not attract mosses unless they are specially coated.

Fibreglass features are also less expensive than stone and are considerably lighter, an important consideration on a balcony for example. This material is adaptable enough to give a fair imitation of real stone – sometimes it is coated with pulverized stone – and works particularly well when it comes to prefabricated waterfalls, streams, cascades and millstones.

Tough, moulded plastic is the cheapest option. This material tends to be used for watercourses, streams, falls and cascades. It requires some disguise in the form of strategically placed rocks, pebbles and gravel because it does not have a very realistic finish.

Those with a stream in their garden can add to its charms with a rustic bridge (above).

Wall-mounted fountains often issue from the mouths of lions (below). Usually, the water drops into a wall basin for recycling; here, it runs over a ledge into a brick pool.

other option is to make your own. This requires some D.I.Y. skill and careful research. The advantages of making your own are that designs can be more flexible and real stones will attract mosses and lichens in time, giving a natural, organic look.

The last few years have seen tremendous advances in the development of kits. Designs have become more sophisticated so that there are styles to suit almost every taste and requirement.

Self-contained fountain kits are ideal for the enthusiastic amateur. They are relatively easy to install as they do not need plumbing in to mains supplies; they recycle their

SPACE SAVERS

If space is at a premium, try a wall-mounted fountain. Typically, these have a stream of water emerging from a decorative feature to fall into a bowl, whence it drains back into the system. These look fine on balconies, in patios, or in a walled, courtyard garden. Typical designs are masks of human or animal heads and flowers.

GARDEN NOTES

An Alpine Bed

Alpines have held a special fascination for generations of gardeners: their delicate beauty can bring enchantment to the smallest garden.

Photos Horticultural

Alpines, as the name suggests, are mountain dwellers. In the wild they grow in the open area above the treeline and below the permanent snowline.

Garden centres, however, now classify as an alpine any plant that has a low, creeping or carpeting habit and the ability to withstand extremes of temperature. Even dwarf trees, such as some conifers, are found in the alpine section.

Alpines are particularly useful in small gardens. They take up very little room but offer a wonderful variety of colours, forms and flowering seasons. Careful selection can ensure that you are rewarded with new delights each season.

Inexperienced gardeners may feel a bit daunted at the prospect of growing alpines, because they have a reputation for being difficult. Some

Serene alpines in a raised bed (above) with dwarf conifers will tempt any gardener. A raised bed is more practical than a rock garden, and allows you to create the effect you want with plants tumbling over the sides.

27

RECOMMENDED VARIETIES

WALL DWELLERS

● Bellflowers such as *Campanula cochleariifolia* or *C. portenschlagiana* make excellent wall dwellers, producing masses of lilac/blue flowers in summer and autumn.
● Some geraniums or cranesbills also do well. Choose *G. dalmaticum* for rich pink flowers in summer; 'Album' is a white variety.
● The fairy foxglove *(Erinus alpinus)* has lovely rose-purple flowers in spring and summer. The 'Albus' variety is pure white.
● Many rockfoils *(Saxifraga* spp.) enjoy life in crevices. Choose *S. callosa lantoscana, S. cotyledon* or *S. longifolia.*

been grown in rock gardens in an attempt to reproduce their mountain habitat. These can be a very attractive feature but there are drawbacks.

Rock gardens can be a very expensive way of growing alpines. Good quality rock is essential, and very costly. All trace of perennial weeds, such as ground elder, must be re-moved from the site and the surrounding area, otherwise your bed will be reduced to a mound of rock and weeds.

Garden balance

A rock garden can be very difficult to work into your garden design. This is especially true if your garden is small, as it may throw everything else out

are, indeed, tricky and require specialized growing techniques. However, there are many varieties that are very accommodating and are simplicity itself to grow.

Golden rules

The first golden rule is that alpines need good drainage. If your soil is a heavy clay, then liberal use of coarse sand and grit is essential.

An alternative is to grow your alpines in some form of container, such as a sink, trough, pot or raised bed. Be generous with crocking material and stand containers on bricks to allow water to drain away freely.

When filling containers, the recipe for success is to add extra grit to good quality potting compost. Or mix your own, using equal parts of good loam, moss peat and coarse grit.

The second golden rule is to choose your site carefully. Although there are varieties that will tolerate some shade, most prefer an open, sunny position. Never make an alpine bed beneath trees.

Alpines have traditionally

Andrew Lawson

of proportion even when sited with care and skill.

There are several exciting and beautiful alternatives to the rock garden. Raised beds make excellent settings for alpines and are easier to maintain as there is less bending. Raising the bed to a height of 45-90cm/18-36in also brings the plants nearer the eye.

Raised beds

One of the beauties of alpines in a raised bed is that you need not restrict yourself to merely planting within the bed; you can plant the sides as well for a really stunning effect.

This is best done at the building stage, though you can plant the sides after building. Roots must be established in the soil so that there are no pockets in which water can

Clusters of the bell-shaped Campanula cochleariifolia 'Oakington Blue' *(opposite top). It is an easy alpine to grow in gardens. A dwarf species with wiry stems, it grows 10-15cm/4-6in high.*

The smaller Erinus alpinus *produces tiny star-shaped, pink flowers (above) which bloom from spring to late summer. They are well-blended here with* Saxifraga, Dianthus *and* Veronica *and are hardy survivors if allowed to grow in a good, sunny position.*

For gardeners with a taste for rarity, Penstemon rupicola *(far left) offers 2.5cm/1in rose-carmine flowers in early summer. A spreading alpine, it does not usually thrive in the wet and does best in sheltered conditions.*

This garden (left) is a gorgeous blend of alpines and conifers, and gives a hint of what can be created in small areas. Alpines always add individuality to their part of a garden.

John Glover/Garden Picture Library

WATER AND FOOD

Always water your alpine plants a couple of hours before planting out.

Water alpine beds in dry weather and feed with a half-strength liquid fertilizer.

Apply bone meal to established beds in early spring.

During warm weather, it is essential to water alpines regularly, even in the evenings (right). During cool spells and in winter, the compost needs only to be kept moist. Watering can be increased if there is early growth. Alpines such as **Primula cortusoides** *(below) need a soil rich in humus.*

collect. Alpine plants will rot if they have soggy roots.

The best material for building a raised bed is local walling stone. Although expensive, it really shows alpines to their best advantage, as it resembles their natural habitat. The colour of the stone provides a wonderful background.

Bed of bricks

The next best building material is weathered bricks. You can disguise their uniform shape by placing some plants close to the sides of the bed so that they creep or trail over the edges. Continue this theme by planting in the walls as you build. When fully established you will have created a breathtaking cascade of flowers and foliage.

Concrete building blocks may be used, but this rather harsh material will also need softening in exactly the same way as the brick-built bed.

Old railway sleepers make a good raised bed but do not allow for planting in the walls. However, trailing plants can help to soften the contours.

Alpine paving

Alpines really come into their own when planted between the slabs of a patio. Many alpines are crevice dwellers and naturally lend themselves to such a scheme. They also stop weeds and grass from invading the cracks.

Choose plants such as saxifrages, cotula, raoulia, phlox and penstemon. See the Project box for details of how to lay an alpine path.

Eric Crichton

Alpine gravel beds (left) are one of the simple alternatives to rock gardens, and are cheaper to create. The material is similar to the worn pebbles used in a shingle bed. Most garden centres will sell gravel which needs to be 30cm/1ft deep for alpine beds, and should have a hardcore layer if there is poor drainage.

PROJECT

AN ALPINE PATH

Marshall Cavendish

1 Fork 5cm/2in of coarse sand into 10cm/4in of soil. Spread the same amount of sand and lay stepping stones on top.

3 Plant the alpines and low-growing herbs suggested for paving. Be sure the plants have room to grow.

2 Space the stones apart, and spread gravel between and alongside them. Keep the gravel firm but light.

4 Add interest to the texture by placing rocks and pebbles alongside the path, even making a tiny wall.

Several low-growing, aromatic herbs, such as thymes, mint and chamomile, may be planted so that they release their rich fragrance as you step on them.

Plant dwarf bulbs in the larger gaps, especially autumn- and winter-flowering varieties to add interest in these 'dead' months. Species iris, tulips, scilla, daffodils and crocus will flourish in a patio. Plant delicate annuals when the bulbs have died back.

Scree and shingle

A scree bed provides an interesting planting scheme. Drainage is all-important. Using a gently sloping site will help if your soil is heavy.

A flat or sunken scree bed may be created in a well-drained area. A good all-purpose mix is of three parts gravel or stone chippings to one part each of loam and peat. Top dress with stone chippings. Only use limestone for lime-loving plants.

A shingle bed is almost identical but the top dressing is well-washed beach pebbles. Extra soil should be incorporated around the roots of plants as you bed them in. The texture of the stones of scree and shingle beds contrasts beautifully with the delicate foliage and flowers of alpine plants.

Making a Rockery

A rockery provides a point of interest in the garden and gives you the chance to be creative with some appealing alpines and garden flowers.

The first garden rockeries were intended to look just like miniature mountains (and some even had models of tweed-clad climbers, complete with ropes), so that the plants in them were completely out of scale. As the idea caught on, rockeries became less fanciful, but were often unimaginative. But nowadays, gardeners have moved away from these unappealing mounds of soil studded with rocks and aubrieta.

Today's rockeries are much more natural-looking, with rocks carefully set into the soil so as to provide the same sort of conditions that rock plants meet in the wild, with horizontal and vertical crevices creating cool, damp places for the plants' roots to run in. The soil has grit added to it, so that it is very well drained, to create a real mountain habitat.

Imitating nature

Alpines make ideal rock plants, but rockeries do not have to be inspired by the Alps. The mountainous areas of Britain, or indeed any high ground with rocky outcrops, can provide a model, as can screes which have become greened over with plants on the lower slopes.

The secret of success is to imitate nature, so that you create a true home for mountain plants, which will then grow and flower happily for many years. Of course, the plants you choose should be in scale with your rock garden. You should try to avoid rampant plants that will take over in a small area. It is also best

Pat Brindley

Andrew Lawson

In a well-established rock garden (left), a colourful carpet of spreading flowers all but obscures the rocks. A stone feature, such as a birdbath, in a similar rock is a happy addition.

The low-growing spruce Picea abies 'Pumila' (above) forms rounded evergreen hummocks.

The alpine primula P. auricula (right) is a colourful addition to any rockery, available in shades of blue, red and yellow.

Few natural colours can match the heavenly blue of the gentians. The trumpet gentian (Gentiana acaulis) (below) is easy enough to grow, but can be temperamental, in some years failing to flower at all.

Photos Horticultural

PLANTS FOR ROCK GARDENS

CONIFERS AND SHRUBS

Juniper	*Juniperus communis* 'Compressa'
Silver fir	*Abies balsamea* 'Hudsonia'
Spruce	*Picea abies* 'Pumila'
	P. mariana 'Nana'
Cypress	*Chamaecyparis lawsoniana* 'Minima'
	C. obtusa 'Nana Compacta'
Broom	*Cytisus ardoinii* (alpine broom)
	C. × beanii
Daphne	*D. arbuscula*
	D. blagayana
Heather	*Erica carnea* (alpine heather)
	E. mackaiana
Rock rose	*Helianthemum alpestre*
	H. nummularium
Rhododendron	*R. campylogynum*
	R. radicans
	R. 'Curlew'

FLOWERING BULBS AND CORMS

Anemone	*A. blanda*
Allium	*A. moly*
Glory of the snow	*Chiondoxa sardensis*
	C. luciliae
Cyclamen	*C. coum*
	C. europeum
Snowdrop	*Galanthus nivalis*
Iris	*I. danfordiae*
	I. histrioides
Daffodil	*Narcissus cyclamineus*
	N. juncifolius
Scilla	*S. siberica*
Tulip	*Tulipa tarda*

FLOWERING ROCK PLANTS

Thrift	*Armeria maritima*
Aubrieta	*A. deltoides*
Dwarf campanula	*C. arvatica*
	C. carpatica
Gentian	*Gentiana acaulis*
	G. verna
Cranesbill	*Geranium cinereum*
	G. dalmaticum
Phlox	*P. douglasii*
	P. subulata
Auricula	*Primula auricula* (alpine species)
Saxifrages	*Saxifraga* species and varieties
Thyme	*Thymus* species and varieties

GARDEN FLOWERS FOR ROCKERIES
(late spring and summer flowering)

Ageratum	*Ageratum spp.*
Alyssum	*Alyssum spp.*
Californian poppy	*Eschscholzia californica*
Geum	*Geum spp.*
Candytuft	*Iberis umbellata*
Poached egg plant	*Limnanthes douglasii*
Mesembryanthemum	*Mesembryanthemum spp.*
Forget-me-not	*Myosotis spp.*

to choose a variety of mountain plants – it is a waste of a rockery to use it just for heathers.

Rock gardens, despite being mini-mountain habitats, can come in all sorts of styles. There is such a wide variety of plants and shrubs, including evergreens, and flowering plants for all seasons, in all shapes and sizes, that you can make your mini-garden very individual. The style you choose will depend both on the layout of the rest of the garden and on what other features you may want to add.

Special features

You may want the rockery to include a pond, perhaps with a watercourse and even a fountain. Oddly enough, although a fountain is an entirely artificial feature, fountains always seem in keeping with the most naturalistic of rockeries.

One reason for the popularity of the rockery/water feature combination is that you can use the soil dug out for the pond to give the rock garden the height it needs. However, if you do this you should be very careful not to create a dull-looking mound, which can happen all too easily.

If you have a natural bank in your garden you are lucky,

Photos Horticultural

Rockeries are usually placed at the side or the back of a garden, against a wall or fence, but this is not a hard and fast rule. A rockery may act as a foreground to the rest of the garden, with a lawn flowing around it (above). Here, a mixed planting of alpines and conifers gives colour and height without having to pile up rocks.

An alternative solution for those who do not want to lift heavy loads is to use hollow artificial rocks (right). Though conveniently and naturalistically shaped, these manufactured rocks do not weather as well as some natural stone.

Collections/Patrick Johns

RECOMMENDED ROCKS

Sandstone A sympathetic, soft-edged rock that weathers well and looks attractive. There are many kinds, nearly all of which are good.

Limestone is an ideal rock, and most limestones weather beautifully. If you choose a hard one, you will still be able to grow lime-hating plants. Limestone 'paving' is natural, weathered limestone, formed during the Ice Age, and a vital home for rare wild flowers. It is not environmentally friendly to buy this type of stone for your garden.

Tufa is a very soft limestone into which alpines can be planted directly, and is perhaps the best of all for rock gardens, but is very expensive indeed. To do it credit you need to be an alpine expert.

Local stones such as Yorkshire stone, millstone and gritstone, are attractive, and are often sold in garden centres for crazy paving. Being in such flat pieces they make rockery building easy on the back and produce a fine, natural effect.

CHOOSING ROCKS

Good rock is nearly always expensive, but you are making a permanent feature and an attractive addition to your garden, so it is well worth spending out on good materials. Do not make the mistake of buying enormous pieces of rock, even if you want to create a dramatic cliff-face. It is always better to use two or three medium rocks rather than one huge one, and plant up the crevices between them. It is best, if possible, to choose a type of rock that is found locally in your area, for a natural effect.

It makes practical sense to construct a pond and a rockery at the same time, and placing two or three rocks around the edges of the pond helps to draw the two features together into a single harmonious design (left).

Limestone (below) is the best rock for a rock garden; it comes in a variety of colours, from pure white through every imaginable shade of cream, buff and grey, and weathers both along and at right angles to the strata.

as this is ideal for a rock garden. Here you can have great fun with rocks without having to move masses of soil. On the other hand, making a rockery in a normal, flat garden need not involve too much digging, as small outcrops can be made on flat ground without too much difficulty.

You dig out a wide, shallow depression and pile the soil behind it, moulded so that it is higher in the middle and tapers to the sides. The rise can then become a rock face, perhaps just 60cm/2ft high and, say, 3.5m/12ft wide. This is a very good way of turning a boringly flat lawn into an undulating, interesting one.

Where to put a rockery

Once you have decided on the shape and size of your rock garden, there are some other important decisions to be made. You may have a general idea where you want it, but there are factors that you must take into consideration. Rockeries should, where possible, be in sun. But you could create a rockery as an integral feature of the garden so that where it runs into shade it changes into a mini-woodland garden or even a bog. A rockery does not have to stand on its own as a naked garden feature; indeed the best gardens are those where each element merges with the next.

Although it should be in the sun, a well-built rockery will have its own shady areas, created by the way the rocks are arranged. Some of these will provide quite deep shade, while others will allow plants to have just a little shade in the middle of the day. The flatter, higher areas will, of course, be in full sun.

Good drainage

Drainage is extremely important for rock garden plants and it is no good trying to make a rockery if the ground under it is waterlogged. Even if you build up over it using imported soil, it never seems to work satisfactorily; so it is much better either to have the ground drained properly or to dig out a bed at least 45cm/18in deep and fill it with plenty of good drainage material to

DIFFICULT ROCKS

Granite is hard, and extremely heavy. It can be used if flattish pieces 30cm/1ft across or less can be found, but it takes skill to create a natural effect with granite. In any case, it is often difficult to obtain.

Gypsum This is the glaringly white 'rockery stone' that comes in difficult, lumpy shapes. It never weathers and is unattractive.

provide a base. The soil you use must also have grit added to it to make it drain well.

It is also important not to site your rockery under trees. This stops plants from flourishing, not only because of the shade cast by the trees, but also because it keeps the rain off, with any moisture that does reach the rockery plants falling as heavy drips from the trees.

If you plan to have a pond in your rockery you should decide on the shape of the pond first, and then dig it out. As the soil is thrown up, make sure that

Pat Brindley

PROJECT
BUILDING A ROCK GARDEN

Some planting can be done as you go along. Put a plant's teased-out root ball on one rock and put another on top, then fill with compost. Otherwise, water the rockery well and allow to settle for a few days before planting. You could put a layer of scree or gravel on the slope to protect the collars of the plants and cut down weeding.

1 Set the first rocks very firmly, ramming an 'alpine' compost – one part sand and gravel to three parts soil – between and behind them.

3 The next layer can curve back into the rockery and out almost to meet the first layer. This creates flat pockets for planting.

Marshall Cavendish

2 Curve in the bottom layer so that it creates a natural line rather than a wall. The rocks should slope back so rain runs into, not off, the rockery.

4 Put smaller rocks at the end of each layer. This gives the effect of the rocks disappearing into the soil for a more naturalistic effect.

Peter McHoy

the subsoil (the compacted soil from below the topsoil) is either discarded or spread out in a layer (never a mound) in the area where the rockery is going to be. This is because plants will not grow in subsoil, and setting rocks in it is not easy. If you do not intend to have a pond, you will either have to sculpt your garden into a hollow and use the hollowed-out earth for your rockery, or buy in topsoil.

The next stage is to use the topsoil to make a shallow mound. When the mound has been completed and shaped to your satisfaction, you can begin to place the rocks in it, starting at the bottom and working up, making sure that each rock is so firmly set that you can stand on it without it rocking. About one-third of each rock should be buried, and the rocks should all tilt slightly backwards.

Don Wildridge

Harry Smith Collection

The brightly coloured, zoned flowers **Mesembryanthemum criniflorum** *(above) are an excellent way of introducing summer colour to the rockery.*

Many alpines and other rock plants are spring-flowering. Though you should be sure to include other plants that will give colour and interest through the summer, a rockery can be a stunningly colourful sight in the first flushes of spring (left top).

An alternative to the wild riot of a spring time rockery is to intersperse the flowering alpines with foliage plants (left). The blue-green dwarf cypress **Chamaecyparis lawsoniana 'Minima Glauca'** *and the mid-green spruce* **Picea abies** *provide a context for the white flowers of* **Iberis sempervirens** *and the yellow blooms of the St John's wort,* **Hypericum rhodoppeum.**

Lay the rocks in layers, or strata, just as you see them in nature. Each rock should bear a good relationship to the next and the strata should meet and break here and there, creating flat pockets of soil and interesting shapes. If you use rocks that are fairly flat, you will be able to make a fascinating garden feature without having to build it very high at all. If you have a pond, you can make a cliff at one side of it, and slope the rockery gently down until it merges with the lawn or a border.

Plants to choose

A rock garden plant is any plant that looks 'right' in a rock garden. The plants to grow will depend to an extent on the size of your rockery and the kind of soil you have (for example, some plants prefer limy, alkaline soil and some hate it). Small alpines offer great variety and you can gradually build up a collection of these fascinating plants. On the other hand, there are plenty of other plants that look in keeping and do not grow too high or spread too far.

For the best effect, choose plants in a variety of shapes and heights. If there is a specialist nursery near you, you

will be able to get useful advice, and the best choice of plants, there. Mound-forming and trailing plants can be mixed with miniature perennials, while dwarf shrubs and conifers add interest in larger rockeries.

Miniature bulbs are at home in rockeries of any size; winter-flowering aconites, scilla and small hyacinths for early spring, followed by miniature daffodils, dwarf tulips and then the smallest irises, and fragile autumn crocuses, will give year-round colour.

One of the most common mistakes people make in selecting plants is to choose only spring-flowering ones. Remember that a rockery which is colourful only in spring is a waste of an opportunity. You can have flowers and interest all year round if you are careful.

Scree Beds

Rock and alpine plants will thrive and your garden will gain interest if you take a tip from nature to create a scree bed.

Derek Gould

In nature a scree is a drift of broken rock that has collected over the years at the base of a cliff. Rocks may be in a wide range of sizes from large boulders to small pebbles and even gravel. Scree contains little soil and rain soon drains through it, but nevertheless many plants manage to grow there.

You can copy this idea in your own garden but, of course, on a much smaller scale. Indeed, a scree bed is an ideal feature for the small or medium-sized garden.

A scree bed provides a natural-looking home for rock plants or alpines and is especially suitable for those that like very well-drained soil. You can grow any shape and size of alpine you choose in your scree bed as they are naturally dwarf plants, but it is usual to concentrate on those with a compact hummock- or mound-forming habit. Carpeting or creeping plants are also suitable provided they are not vigorous enough to swamp other plants that are growing nearby.

What is required?

You do not need any special conditions for a scree bed. The soil type or condition does not matter as generally the bed is raised above the level of the surrounding soil.

Choose a very sunny position, however, as most alpines need plenty of sun if they are to grow and flower well. The bed should not be overhung by trees or other plants – site it in a completely open spot.

The style of your house is an indication of whether or not a scree bed is for you. Scree beds look good with modern architecture and indeed are an ideal choice for a contemporary setting. They also look at ease in surburban or town gardens but do not really work well in a cottage or country garden where they tend to look both out of scale and out of character with the rest.

Planting alpines

Make your scree bed more attractive and natural looking by partially sinking a few pieces of rock into the soil. If you can, stick to the same type of rock as you have used for the surrounds. Choose some really well-shaped pieces for a pleasing effect and instal them in groups before you start to

Photos Horticultural

In their natural habitats alpine plants grow on scree beds. They are remarkably well adapted to free-draining, rocky soil, and can survive in dry positions which few other plants could tolerate. There are many alpines, like this sedum spathufolium 'Cape Blanca' (right), which store moisture in their fleshy leaves. The blue-grey sedum blends so well with the rocky background that it could almost be carved out of the stone but the striking star-shaped yellow flowers bring it dramatically back to the forefront.

When creating a scree bed in your garden you should try to simulate the conditions they provide in nature. Whether you are making a raised bed or converting a larger area of the garden (below), ensure it is free-draining and rocky because alpines hate to have their feet wet! If you have the space for a large scree bed disperse the plants evenly. Incorporate a few well-placed rocks and plant the alpines nearby. Include a good mixture of colours, interesting shapes and contrasting textures.

position your plants.

Nestle some of the plants up to the rocks and allow some to grow over them, especially mat-forming kinds like raoulia. As most alpines are small plants, include several of each kind to create a bold effect. Try arranging them in groups of three plants. This may reduce the number of different plants you have room to grow but it will avoid the 'spotty' effect which results when single specimens of a lot of different kinds are planted.

The best planting time for alpines is early to mid-spring. They will establish quickly as the soil will be warming up at this time of year. If you build your scree garden in the autumn or winter and then take the time to plan the range of species you need to achieve the effect you want, you will find that you are ready to start planting in spring.

The best plants

Most of the plants you need will be available from the alpine section of your garden centre. For a wider choice of more unusual plants you can also buy from a mail order alpine-plant specialist.

To ensure your scree bed looks well balanced and has plenty of interesting features choose your plants carefully. Make sure you have a mixture of mat-forming, foliage and feature plants while mound-forming plants and alpines with intricate rosette-shaped foliage can be used to form the focal points of the bed.

When planting, choose the most eye-catching locations for plants you are using as focal points and plant the others around them. Make sure you do not plant carpeters too near your focal points or your prize specimens may be overwhelmed when these spread.

Stork's bill (*Erodium reichardii*) forms a neat mound of foliage and produces white or pink flowers in summer. Rock jasmine (*Androsace sempervivoides*) is an evergreen with foliage which forms a rosette-like symmetrical pattern. It produces pink flowers in the spring and will only grow in very free-draining soil. *Lewisia cotyledon* has similar fleshy foliage and produces flowers in pink or purple on upright stalks in early summer. It grows specially well in a very free-draining soil.

Choose rosettes

Tuft-like cobweb houseleek *Sempervivum arachnoideum* really looks as if spiders have been spinning their webs between the rosetted, succulent leaves. In winter it is covered with white webbing and red flowers appear in summer. Another rosetted alpine grown for its unusual foliage and pretty yellow flowers is *Sedum spathulifolium* 'Cape Blanco'. It is an evergreen and has fleshy, purple-flushed, silvery-

Neil Holmes

Narcissus bulbocodium, or the hoop petticoat (above), is an unusual member of the narcissus family which flowers in late winter or very early spring.

This scree bed (right) is in the best position for flowering alpine plants as it enjoys full sun.

Lewisia cotyledon (below) loves a well-drained, sunny spot and so is an ideal plant for a scree bed. Here it is flourishing, growing out of a natural stone wall.

green leaves all year round.

Edelweiss is a favourite alpine plant and its star-shaped, felted white flowers are so pretty it should be placed in a prominent position. The woolly grey leaves form tufts which spread up to 15cm/6in.

Plants with a mat-forming or spreading habit should be planted near rocks so that they can creep over them adding a splash of colour. The bellflower, *Campanula pulla*, is a mat-forming alpine with tufty foliage which produces dark violet bell-shaped flowers between late spring and early summer. Grow it with the mat-forming alpine pink *Dianthus × arvernensis* which

Pat Brindley

Photos Horticultural

Derek Gould

PRACTICAL POINTS

Unless your soil is very well drained, you will need to create a raised bed about 30cm/12in deep. This can be edged with rocks, or mini drystone walls.

Place a 10cm/4in layer of rubble in the bottom. Top with well-drained compost which you can make from 10 parts pea shingle (or stone chippings), 1 part loam, 1 part peat or peat substitute, 1 part sharp horticultural sand (not builders' sand) and a dash of bone meal. Mix the ingredients well.

Neil Holmes

Sempervivums, or houseleeks, are ideal plants for scree beds, rock gardens and dry walls. Sempervivum arachnoideum (above) is known as the cobweb houseleek as its leaves appear to have a cobweb of fine hairs covering them. It also has attractive flowers.

The alpine primula is another plant which needs a very well-drained soil. Primula allionii (below) is a tiny plant, only 5cm/2in high, which flowers in early spring.

begins to flower in late spring and outlasts the bellflower into late summer. Its pink flowers are delightfully fragrant and it reaches a height and spread of 15cm/6in.

The attractive cup flower *Nierembergia repens* flowers for a long period over the summer. Lovely white bell-shaped flowers face the sun and grow out of a mat of glossy green foliage. Cinquefoil (*Potentilla cuneata*) produces yellow flowers in summer and catchfly (*Silene schafta*) has bright magenta-rose flowers between

With scree beds less is often best. A few well placed boulders and some simple plants create a look which is tranquil and serene, and all the elements of the garden balance beautifully. The bamboo fence adds a hint of the orient and the modern bench complements the artistic sophistication. Hostas, conifers, grasses and some achilleas for colour thrive on the free-draining soil conditions that the scree bed provides.

Harry Smith Collection

late spring and late autumn.

St John's wort, *Hypericum olympicum,* is a shrubby plant which makes an interesting change from the more familiar succulent alpines. It produces bright yellow flowers in summer and has a height and spread of 15cm/6in.

For all year round foliage interest plant *Raoulia australis,* an evergreen mat-forming foliage plant with tiny grey-green leaves. It grows to only 1cm/½in high but spreads to 25cm/10in.

Finishing touches

When you have finished planting, the soil surface can be covered with a thin layer – no more than 1cm/½in – of pea shingle. Pea shingle is readily available from builders' merchants and garden centres. Even better would be a layer of stone chippings, which are sometimes available in bags at garden centres and almost certainly at stone merchants. Coarse grit, also available in bags at garden centres, is another attractive alternative.

This layer of shingle, grit or chippings serves a number of

P ROJECT

PLANTING IN ROCKS

A novel idea for a scree bed is a rock with little alpines actually growing from within it.

Try to find a rock with plenty of cracks and crevices in which to plant. A popular type of rock for planting is a soft limestone known as tufa. This is so soft that planting holes can be made in it very simply with a hammer and cold chisel but always wear some form of eye protection. The rock should be sunk into the soil by about one third.

Small alpines suitable for such a scheme include saxifraga and sempervivum and also the horned campion, Physoplexis comosa (Phytenma comosum) with its bottle-shaped flowers.

Photos Horticultural

● Make the cracks or holes quite deep and angled towards the centre of the rock. If you want to enlarge them use a cold chisel and club hammer, but be fairly gentle or you could split the rock in two!

● Partially fill the holes or cracks with a gritty potting compost, such as John Innes No. 1 with some extra grit added. Poke it well down with a blunt-ended stick.

● Remove each plant from its pot and gently push rootball into the hole or crack until it touches the compost. Add more compost around it and firm moderately.

● Thoroughly water the planted rock, then water regularly in dry weather as plants must not be allowed to dry out.

SHORT CUTS

A GROUND-LEVEL BED

A raised bed is not necessary if you have extremely well-drained soil, such as one which is naturally gravelly. Simply section off an area which you want to devote to alpines and then plant directly in the soil. Water plants well for the first few days.

purposes: most importantly it gives the scree bed a natural-looking appearance. Also, it ensures very good drainage around the plants so that water cannot accumulate and cause them to rot around the necks, prevents the soil from drying out rapidly in hot weather and stops weeds and unwanted seedlings from growing too quickly.

Watch those weeds

Once you have given the plants the conditions they enjoy your scree bed will need very little attention. One exception to this is in very hot weather. Although the plants need very well-drained soil this does not mean they should be allowed to suffer from water shortage. Make sure that during dry periods in the summer you water the scree bed thoroughly, ideally with a garden sprinkler. The occasional weed should be carefully dug out to avoid disturbing the alpines. Be especially vigilant about removing perennial weeds while they are still small. If any do become established in with your plants, paint them with a spot weed-killer, being careful to avoid the leaves of the other plants. Alternatively, dig up both the weed and the plant and remove the weed roots before replacing the plant. To keep everything looking neat and tidy trim off dead blooms when flowering is over.

After a number of years the plants may start to become overcrowded. Lift them out carefully in early to mid-spring. Split them into a number of smaller portions, discarding the centre of each, and replant them.

Although scree beds tend to suit modern architecture, with the right choice of plants they can also add a touch of cottage garden charm. Perfectly placed by a patio (below) this scree bed makes an excellent transitional area between the paving slabs and the flower bed at the rear. Digitalis purpurea, the common English foxglove, stands tall, and graces the garden with its delicate pink, purple and cream spotted flowers.

PERFECT PLANTS

The following are easy and popular plants for a scree bed and should be available from a well-stocked garden centre. Order more unusual plants from a specialist nursery.

- rock pink *(Dianthus × arvernensis) (above)*
- storksbill *(Erodium reichardii)*
- St John's wort *(Hypericum olympicum)*
- saxifrage *(Saxifraga × apiculata)*
- stonecrop *(Sedum spathulifolium* 'Cape Blanco')
- cinquefoil *(Potentilla cuneata)*

Making a Sunken Garden

The ideal way to landscape a natural hollow, a sunken garden can also improve a flat site by adding a change of level, privacy and shelter.

Sunken gardens have a magic of their own. Sitting in one, you can relax in your own private suntrap, sheltered from wind, traffic noise and other people. The best of them are real secret gardens.

Sunken gardens were common features in formal and semi-formal gardens 50 years ago. The traditional sunken garden was a round or square area several feet lower than the surrounding garden. Plants were grown in the stone walls or rockeries shoring up the sides, and there was a lawn, a seat and perhaps a formal pond in the centre.

Informality

Sunken gardens do not have to be formal. The basic idea behind a sunken garden is to plant up a hollow in the

Harry Smith Collection

A sunken garden can be a central feature or it can be subtly blended in. If your sunken garden has lots of 'hard landscaping' – walls and beds of brick or stone, floors of paving or concrete – it will stand out more (above), at least until the materials have weathered. The sunken garden (right) blends in, although it has steps and flooring of paving stones, because the beds at the sides are a continuation of the surrounding lawn.

Peter McHoy

A traditional, formal garden (above) is in the grounds of a manor house. The entire sunken area is surrounded by tall hedges with a row of pleached limes (their branches have been interwoven) at one end. The sunken area is on three levels, with lawns and beds. Steps lead to a central pond via a path flanked by box topiary.

Stone walling, here with a brick coping (below), blends well into a garden. This small gully within the garden has been accentuated by mounding the beds up to its edges.

ground. This can suit many different styles of garden.

You could include a small sunken area within an informal or even a wild garden. And a tiny town garden tucked in between tall buildings gives an illusion of being sunken, due to its surroundings.

Siting sunken gardens

All it takes is a little imagination and a few ideas to transform your 'problem' patch into a positive benefit!

It is important to choose a well drained site for a sunken garden, otherwise it can end up being awash all winter.

The best sites are raised up above the level of surrounding land, perhaps within a mound or on a slope. Gravelly or sandy soil is an advantage and the garden should be in a sunny, sheltered area.

Avoid trying to make a sunken garden on heavy clay soil and in places with a high water table, unless you want a bog garden. Check by digging a hole in winter – if it fills with water that doesn't run away, the chances are that you have a high water table.

Traditional style

The traditional, formal sunken garden was situated towards the middle of a larger semi-formal garden, surrounded by grass and paths and by a wall or shrubberies.

To get into the garden, you went down a short flight of steps, and the walls of the sunken area would be of stone or brick. The floor of the garden would have been closely mown grass. In the centre was a round or square pond, with perhaps a fountain or statue, and there were formal beds of annuals or low perennials.

You can recreate this and perhaps make it into a whole garden – it looks good in a small courtyard behind an older town house.

Try adding a formal topiary tree, either in the ground or in a pot, and a seat on some paving slabs. Edging flower beds with dwarf box looks good.

A paved garden

Slightly formal, a paved sunken garden could occupy an entire courtyard behind a town house, or a small front garden. It could also be an isolated feature within a larger garden.

Simply pave the area with bricks, cobbles or slabs, using a pattern that emphasizes the shape of the courtyard. In a round garden, for instance, lay bricks in concentric rings.

CREATING A FORMAL SUNKEN GARDEN

- Choose a circular, oval, square or oblong shape.
- Make it 1.5-1.8m/5-6ft deep, so that your head is below ground level when seated. If the hollow is shallower, add a low wall or hedge around the outside.
- Reinforce the inside of the sunken area with walls of stone or brick.
- For a semi-formal garden, you could make the side walls gently sloping, lined with rockery stone.
- Ensure good drainage in the floor of the garden if you are planting it up. Dig the garden 30cm/12in deeper than you need, then place 5cm/2in of gravel over a 15cm/6in layer of coarse rubble, before replacing a good layer of topsoil.

Tania Midgley

Neil Holmes

Derek Gould

Neil Holmes

Add a seat and, round the edge, a low wall or shrubs. Groups of interestingly shaped plants, such as phormium or hardy yucca (*Yucca filamentosa*), will create interest.

A sunken garden in a sunny spot is just the place for rock plants. Either plant them in the dry stone walls that line the sides of a garden, or replace one or all of the walls with a gently sloping rockery.

Rock gardens

Plant sun-loving species in walls that get sun for at least half the day. Reserve small hardy ferns and crevice-dwelling shade-lovers, like ramonda and haberlea, for the north-facing side.

You can pave the floor of the garden, or make a series of gravel paths between raised beds or small, natural-looking rocky outcrops. You could also add a seat on a small area of paving, with a collection of sink gardens nearby.

Mediterranean style

Mediterranean herbs, silver leaved perennials and slightly tender plants, such as perennial salvias, gazanias, osteospermum, pelargoniums and many other brightly coloured species, all do well in a sunny sunken garden. The more tender species, such as gazanias and pelargoniums, will, however, need to be overwintered in a frost-free place.

The style can be formal or informal, depending on how you lay it out.

Whichever you choose, remember that these kinds of plants need good drainage. Plant them in the walls or sloping rockery, in raised beds or in urns or other containers, rather than in the ground.

Use paving or gravel for the garden floor – the reflected heat and light are beneficial.

Wild gardens

A sunken wild garden should be very natural in style. It could be crammed full of flowers, with just the odd path wending its way through. And there might be a tiny clearing of shredded bark with a fallen log to sit on.

Or you could have a wild-flower lawn. Choose species that thrive in moist conditions

Pat Brindley

A BOG GARDEN

A bog garden is the ideal way to plant up a sunken garden on wet soil. Go for a natural style and use moisture-loving plants such as *Inula, Buphthalmum*, candelabra primula, *Iris laevigata* hybrids, the corkscrew rush (*Juncus effusus* 'Spiralis'), mimulus, marsh marigold and purple loosestrife.

GOING FOR AN INFORMAL STYLE

● Leave natural hollows unaltered as far as possible.
● Choose a simple, flowing shape when creating an artificial hollow.
● Avoid fussy shapes with lots of convolutions, or the edges of the garden are likely to be weak.
● Make the sides slope gently; this looks more natural and they are much easier to plant.
● Reinforce sides with rockery stones or dry stone walling. You can also terrace them, making a series of level beds, each with a low retaining wall.
● Reinforce the rim of the garden with paving over proper foundations, well concreted in place. Alternatively, plant heavily round the rim to deter people from walking too close to the edge.
● Aim for a slightly uneven floor, rather than one which is entirely flat, and therefore unnatural looking.

Gazanias (opposite top) will bring a vivid splash of colour to a corner of your sunken garden. Except in very mild areas, they are best treated as annuals. This variety is Gazania 'Freddie'.

Salvias (left) are members of the sage family. The many varieties include annuals, biennials, perennials and even evergreen shrubs. They have showy flowers and are ideal for a bed in a sunken garden. This one is Salvia sylvestris 'Mainacht'.

Whether your sunken garden is formal, as here (above), or informal, it should have a comfortable bench or seat in a sunny corner out of the wind.

If your entire garden is on a slope, or you have a slope within the garden, you can create a sunken garden within a natural fold of the land (right).

if the base of your sunken garden is wet in winter. Around this you might have slightly raised flower beds edged with logs, containing taller species arranged naturally in clumps.

If you have a large, dell-like hollow, gently sloping grass banks could lead into the garden, with a choice of paths winding their way down. Plant the bends with drifts of tall flowers, such as rosebay willowherb, or with native bushes like *Viburnum opulus*, so that the view below reveals itself gradually.

A sunken garden should be a private haven and a restful place which is always a delight to visit.

A Mediterranean Garden

Simple alterations – white paint, terracotta pots, gravel and a few exotic plants – can evoke the atmosphere of the sun-drenched Mediterranean in your garden.

Eric Crichton

Differences in culture and climate have produced a distinctly different style of gardening around the Mediterranean. It is, though, a style that can, with a few adaptations, be applied in temperate climates. It's not at all difficult to do, and is ideally suited to the small spaces that most of us have nowadays. Or, less ambitiously, you could give just part of your garden the Mediterranean treatment – perhaps the front-of-house area, or the patio.

What exactly is a Mediterranean garden? Individual gardens vary, of course, but as you may know from Continental holidays, they are often quite formal in character, with geometric shapes – square, rectangular or round beds, and straight paths – rather than the undulations and curves usually recommended by British garden designers.

The lawn is conspicuous by its absence, for the purely practical reason that grass does not grow lush and green without lavish amounts of rain – it would be brown for most of the summer. Gravel and paving take the place of grass, allowing paths to be integrated with open areas around the beds and creating a spacious feel even in tiny plots.

Sun traps

Many such gardens are sun traps, enclosed by high white walls, characteristically capped with curved red tiles (pantiles), and often pierced by archways offering tantalizing

White walls and red pantiles, clusters of containers brimming with annuals, sparkling gravel and cool conifers; all these things speak of Mediterranean heat, yet this garden has been created in temperate southern England.

glimpses of what lies beyond.

Other typical features are masses of pelargoniums, tumbling from a balcony or planted in ornate terracotta pots, small formal pools and fountains, spiky architectural plants like yuccas and phormiums, and column-shaped trees, especially dark cypress, which make dramatic accents against a clear blue sky.

Enclosures

If your garden is walled, or part walled, you are off to a flying start. Paint boundary walls with two or three coats of white exterior grade emulsion, and if possible lay red pantiles along the top – these are available from most builder's merchants.

Unless recently creosoted, fencing can be painted white with water-based paint designed for use on timber. The effect will not be quite the same, but white paint will give you the extra light-reflectance essential for a sunny feel.

Traditional privet hedges are not really in style, but a conifer one, especially if dark, might look just right. If you already have a privet hedge, clip it closely and often for a formal look; if you are feeling particularly ambitious, you could start training it into a

Photos Horticultural

Pat Brindley

GARDEN NOTES

PERFUMED GARDEN

Do not forget to include fragrance in your Mediterranean garden. Plant thyme, marjoram and rosemary, whose scent is redolent of hillsides all over France, Italy and Greece. To get maximum fragrance, put them in a sunny spot backed by heat-retaining paving or rocks.

Choose strongly scented shrubs like lilac, philadelphus and Mexican orange blossom (*Choisya ternata*) and fragrant varieties of rose.

The right plants can add to the impression of warmth. Hot bright colours – reds, oranges and yellows – are the best choice for bedding plants and annuals. Free-flowering plants such as petunias and pelargoniums, especially when they are displayed against white walls and light gravels, give the best effect (above).

Other suitable container subjects are exotic, succulent plants such as the agaves. This one (left) is 'Variegata', a variety of the century plant (A. americana).

MINI-MEDITERRANEAN

To give a dark courtyard or semi-basement area the Mediterranean look, first lighten the overall colour. Paint walls white and clean existing paving with powerful quarry tile cleaner (from builder's merchants), or put down gravel or new slabs in a light colour. Use a mixture of 50:50 bleach and water to scrub green slime from brickwork. Prune and thin trees to get in more light and cover eyesores with white-painted trellis. Fill with bright-coloured annuals and evergreen architectural plants in terracota pots.

Photos Horticultural

geometric topiary shape.

Another possibility is to create a new wall across the garden to define your Mediterranean area. Use concrete walling blocks, rendered and topped with pantiles, to a height of 1.8m/6ft. For a Spanish look, use decorative pierced blocks.

If you cannot do any of these things, just paint the lower part of the house wall white — fake or real shutters added to the windows add to the Mediterranean look.

Gardens in the Mediterranean are thought of as outdoor rooms, and the authentic look requires furnishing (right). A sunshade is de rigeur, even if not strictly necessary in the local climate.

Scent is as important as colour; the flowers and foliage of **Lonicera** *japonica 'Aureoreticulata' (below) provide both, even in a shady, north-facing spot.*

Photos Horticultural

Gravel has a hot, dry look reminiscent of poor Mediterranean soils and sparkles in the sun. It is also very practical, providing a clean, free-draining surface to walk on at little cost. Choose a pale, neutral-coloured gravel for a natural look and maximum light reflectance.

Provided the soil is treated with weedkiller first, or the gravel laid over polythene, an annual application of path weedkiller should keep it completely weed-free. Lay the gravel at least 5cm/2in thick, to replace grass and to make straight paths and rectangular shapes. Confine it with bricks, edging slabs or timber so that it does not disappear into the surrounding soil.

Paving is more expensive than gravel, but many gardens already have a small paved area at the back of the house, which could be extended. Again, if the paving is informal in shape, relay it in a more formal design.

Some kind of water feature is an essential part of any Mediterranean garden, preferably one including a simple fountain to provide the soothing sound of falling water.

If you already have a pool, and it is the usual natural or kidney shape, remake it in a round, rectangular or octagonal design. A central fountain in a classical style would provide the finishing touch.

If creating a pool from scratch, make it a formal one with raised sides built of concrete facing blocks or bricks. On a more modest level, you could install a wall fountain or a bird bath of formal design, positioned so that it will make a focal point.

Planting

The plants in your Mediterranean garden do not necessarily have to belong to that region — the first rule of successful gardening, as ever, is to grow what will flourish in your micro-climate and soil. Keep most of what you have, but arrange it differently, and punctuate it with unusual and striking plants that are often found in hotter climates.

Divide up a conventional, meandering herbaceous border into neat geometrical shapes; raised beds, created with low walls or railway sleepers, are ideal for this. Plant the beds densely, including as many silver-grey-leaved and spiky plants as you can. Sea holly (*Eryngium*), giant thistle (*Onopordum*) and *Cineraria maritima* will all fill the bill.

For the sub-tropical effect, add a few architectural foliage plants such as century plants (*Agave*), New Zealand flax (*Phormium tenax*) and yuccas. Semi-hardy palms are also good – look for European fan palm (*Chamaerops humilis*), windmill palm (*Trachycarpus fortunei*) and Washington palm (*Washingtonia filifera*).

Containers

Always have plenty of plants in containers, preferably ones made of terracotta or stone, especially around a paved area. Some of these can be used for architectural plants, to provide a focus of interest just where you want it. This

Photos Horticultural

LOTS OF POTS

Masses of containers bursting with summer flowers are essential to the Mediterranean garden, and much the easiest thing to copy. Use everything you can get hold of:
- Ornate terracotta pots (expensive) or cheaper plastic ones.
- Imitation stone tubs and window boxes with relief ornamentation.
- Large tins and plastic cartons, old washing up bowls, plastic buckets – paint black or white.
- Old car tyres, pulled inside out and painted white, or a grey colour to simulate lead.
- Ancient kitchen sinks.
- Window boxes and hanging baskets for colour at higher levels.

DON'T FORGET!

The spiky leaves of yuccas add an authentically exotic architectural note to a Mediterranean garden. Some species have a basal rosette of spiky leaves; others, such as Spanish dagger (Y. gloriosa) carry them in tufts on unbranched stems (above). These are 'Variegata', with golden margins to their leaves.

French marigolds (Tagetes patula) are excellent container subjects, and will bring a splash of hot colour to a sunny spot (right). Here, the colours are cooled by a variegated hosta and a blue lobelia.

Pat Brindley

also makes it easy to move tender plants inside during the winter, though beware of using containers so large you cannot shift them when they are full of earth.

Hot flowers

For summer bedding, use the hottest, strongest colours you can find – scarlet, yellow and shocking pink rather than pastels and blues. Nasturtiums, French marigolds, petunias and salvias all come in the right bold colours, but above all make good use of bedding geraniums (pelargoniums). Al-

though they may not flower quite as exuberantly as they do in the hot Mediterranean sun, the new F1 varieties in particular, planted in warm sheltered spots, will put up a wonderful show lasting until the first frosts. Always include plenty of the cascading or ivy-leaved varieties which will tumble abundantly over the edges of containers, just as they do in Italy.

To clothe the walls, use some of the more exotic

Formal hedging can find its place in a Mediterranean garden (top). In this Italian garden, an arch has been cut from a tall hedge to create a bower. This provides both a cool place to sit and a dark area, framed in green, against which to view the sunlit plants.

The lovely flowers of the deciduous trumpet vine (Campsis radicans) appear in late summer (above).

climbers such as passion flower (*Passiflora caerulea*), which is evergreen, with large mauve and white flowers; or trumpet vine (*Campsis*), which is deciduous, with spectacular, orange-red, trumpet-shaped flowers.

High walls inevitably bring shade for part of the day. In these areas use plants with golden or gold-splashed leaves, such as *Elaeagnus*, *Euonymous* and *Hosta fortunei* 'Aureomarginata', to create an illusion of sunlight. A small, golden-leaved conifer is ideal for brightening a dark corner all year round. Similarly, clothe a north-facing wall with the evergreen honeysuckle *Lonicera japonica* 'Aureoreticulata', which has bright green leaves netted with gold.

Suitable trees

A Mediterranean garden is above all sunny, so avoid large trees that cast a lot of shade. An existing one should be

professionally thinned and reduced in height to let in more light. Flowering cherries are very suitable, giving you early spring blossom and remaining fairly compact. *Prunus* 'Amanogawa' is especially good for a tiny garden, as its branches all point upwards, like those of a poplar.

Any small, upright-growing conifer will add the right touch in summer and winter too – but beware the giants. The Italian cypress whose pencil-like outline and deep green, almost black, aromatic foliage is such a feature of the Mediterranean scene is *Cupressus sempervirens* 'Stricta'. It should not grow more than about 4.5m/15ft high.

A feature of larger Mediterranean gardens is a paved area covered by a pergola and sometimes partially enclosed with pillars and low walls or trellis. The disadvantage with these in less sunny climates is that they will probably cast more shade than is desirable for all but a very few days in the year. However, if you erect a pergola in a place that is already shaded you have nothing to lose, and the effect, once the bare wood is clothed with a grape vine, roses or jasmine, is instantly Continental.

Always use planed timber to build such structures in the Mediterranean garden, as rustic poles or their like detract from the formal look.

Furniture

As the Mediterranean garden is usually viewed as an outdoor room, garden furniture is essential. For a Continental look, choose chairs and small tables made in aluminium but using traditional cast-iron designs. An alternative is the painted, slatted, wooden designs reminiscent of French parks. Existing timber garden seats can be painted white.

Picnic tables with integral benches are really a North American invention, but blend in quite well. A true Mediterranean garden more often features an incredibly ancient, knocked together, wooden table, proudly bearing the ring marks and scars of countless *al fresco* meals.

Table umbrellas and window awnings are much used in a genuine Mediterranean garden – although rarely necessary in the British climate, they help to create the right look.

The half-hardy annual Salvia splendens blazes with fiery colour in the late summer and early autumn. The species is a solid red, but some varieties are bi-coloured, while others, such as 'Phoenix Mixed' (right) boast shades of pink and purple.

Photos Horticultural

Paving is an acceptable alternative to gravel, especially when it is of a light-coloured stone (below). Here the Mediterranean ambience is heightened by the style of the house, with its white walls, pantiles, louvred shutters, and wrought iron balcony, as well as a colourful collection of Impatiens spilling out of their containers.

Photos Horticultural

LET THERE BE LIGHT

Mediterranean gardens are meant to be enjoyed after dark as well as in the daytime, and outdoor lighting adds the final touch. Where a patio adjoins the house, have an exterior light fitting on the wall, connected to the mains. Otherwise use low-voltage light fittings running off a transformer plugged into the mains.

BRIGHT IDEAS

An Oriental Garden

Oriental gardens, though far removed from their Western equivalents, are full of ideas for creating beautiful, serene effects in a limited space.

The oriental gardener creates effects by playing on the textures and subtle shadings of foliage (above and facing page). Natural materials such as stones and pebbles are chosen to enhance the natural effect and for their symbolic value.

Elizabeth Whiting

The sublime tranquillity of the oriental garden is no accident. The extraordinary peacefulness that pervades every leaf and stone, enhanced by subtle colour, uncluttered plantings and a wonderful sense of space, is generated by using some simple but highly-disciplined design principles.

It is the achievement of generations of religious and philosophical thought far removed from Western ideas, but with a similar aim. Both East and West seek restful surroundings as a retreat from the bustle of daily life, especially that of a busy, urban environment. We share a love of nature's beauty, recreating it in our gardens to restore the spirit and give enjoyment to ourselves and our friends.

But, while Western gardens are often an abundance of crammed colour celebrating nature's variety, the Chinese or Japanese gardener attempts to recreate the magnificence of the natural landscape with the simplicity of an oriental painting.

In the garden, every detail – the line of a single branch, the moss on a stone, the glint of water through leaves – symbolizes a different aspect of the natural world. Each element is carefully chosen according to a strict code laid down over generations. The vastness and variety of the natural landscape can be suggested in a manner as simple as the Japanese dry gardens of rock and sand, and in the smallest of spaces, down to a perfect miniature garden in a bowl.

Over the threshold

In the oriental world, the sanctity of the home is paramount. The house and garden are treated as one, linked by a covered veranda with no balustrade which opens the living-rooms to the garden and allows it to be viewed from a slightly elevated position.

The Chinese philosophy of *yin-yang* (known as *in-yo* in Japan) sees the world as the expression of harmony between contrasts; between light, strength and masculinity on the one hand, and twilight, delicacy and femininity on the other. So in the garden, it is essential to retain a balance between such contrasting ele-

Floral colour is used for an accent in oriental gardens. Water hawthorn (Eichhornia crassipes, right) adds colour to pools with its spikes of lilac or blue summer flowers. A floating plant, it increases rapidly and can prove invasive, though it is generally checked by frost.

RECOMMENDED PLANTS

When choosing plants for an oriental-style garden, consider their contribution to subtle contrasts of texture, building light and shade, balancing vertical and horizontal lines and, above all, retaining an uncluttered elegance.

Trees are often placed singly to make the most of their individual characteristics. Varieties of Japanese maple (*Acer palmatum*) are chosen for beauty of form and leaf and autumn colour, including the delicate texture of 'Dissectum'. Flowering cherry (*Prunus*) provides spring blossom and autumn colour. *P. sargentii* is slow-growing, but will, after many years, reach some 8m/25ft – 'Accolade' is a smaller hybrid. *P.* 'Shimidsu Sakura' is widely-branching, reaching about 3m/10ft. Pines and conifers are chosen for evergreen foliage. The mountain pine (*Pinus mugo*), growing to about 2m/6ft, has an interesting spreading habit with a rather tangled appearance, evocative of the natural landscape.

Foliage Bamboos may be too vigorous for small gardens, but try *Pleioblastus viridistriatus* (syn. *Arundinaria viridistriata*), with its 1-1.5m/3-5ft purple stems and yellow-striped leaves. Blue fescue (*Festuca glauca*) and golden *Hakonechloa macra* 'Aureola' are excellent grasses. For ferns, try *Adiantum pedatum* (the Northern maidenhair fern) and *A. venustum,* both with beautifully delicate fronds – these prefer neutral to acid soil. Hostas provide good sculptural foliage, while box (*Buxus sempervirens*) can be clipped into neat boulder-like domes. For authentic effects, allow mosses and lichens some freedom. Otherwise, substitute Mind-your-own-business (*Soleirolia soleirolii* syn. *Helxine soleirolii*), or carpeting alpines such as *Saxifraga moschata* 'Cloth of Gold', which will bring light, golden touches to shadier spots.

Flowering plants such as azalea, rhododendron, camellia, iris, peony, chrysanthemum and Japanese quince (*Chaenomeles speciosa*) are used selectively.

Water plants The grass-like leaves of *Typha minima* contrast well with water lilies (*Nymphaea*) and the invasive, but frost tender water hyacinth (*Eichhornia crassipes*).

The simple principles of oriental garden design can be scaled down and adapted to some unusual sites (left). Here, a corner of a city rooftop has been screened off and a young, container-grown Japanese larch (Larix kaempferi) has been 'underplanted' with a variegated ivy and tubs containing Fatsia japonica and an azalea. Large, water-smoothed stones complete the picture. This pleasing arrangement depends on the fast-growing larch being pruned regularly; left to its own devices it matures into a very tall tree.

ments as light and shade, angular and curved contours, and stone and water.

Since the natural landscape has no rigid boundaries, different devices are used to obscure the limits of the garden and increase the sense of space.

Dense plantings, often with conifers, mask the fence, and are glimpsed through the branches of trees with more open habits and lighter foliage, such as flowering cherries, which are planted nearer the house. Elements from neighbouring gardens become part of the picture, continuing the landscape beyond the fence, while pathways meander through the garden, twisting away out of sight into an imaginary distance.

Planned informality

The regularity and symmetry of Western formal gardens are disliked in the East. The oriental gardener admires instead the irregular in all its variety, symbolizing the uncertainty of nature. Great delight is taken in the weathered surface of a stone, the asymmetrical arrangement of a few plants or boulders, and in the positioning of a tree so that a branch partially hides some other feature of the garden.

Natural harmony

Above all, the gardener must work in harmony with nature itself. Even fences, which enclose the entire garden for privacy, must be of natural materials – usually bamboo or wood. Where a solid screen is not necessary, they are often of a slightly open pattern, allowing glimpses of greenery beyond the garden.

Stone and water are essential elements, taken direct from the natural landscape. The gardener will search for days for the right stones, delighting most in those from streams or the seashore which reflect the actions of nature in their worn surfaces, and perhaps a partial clothing of moss. Stones are admired for their surface texture and colouring, which change with the rain or sun, and are used for paths, for the edges of ponds or beds or simply for their own sake. Shrubs, ferns and grasses enhance by contrast the character of the stone, emphasizing its strength and mass.

Water may be represented symbolically in stone or sand, or feature in a pond, waterfall,

Varieties of Japanese maple (Acer palmatum 'Dissectum') are ideal for a Japanese-style garden; the purple, divided leaves of 'Atropurpuream' (left) turn red in autumn.

It can take decades, even centuries, to grow miniature trees – bonsai – in a bowl, and their price reflects this, but they are a true ornament to a garden (above).

MINIATURE GARDENS

The ability to express the greatest landscape in the smallest space reaches its peak in the miniature landscapes created within the confines of a single bowl.

These started out as arrangements of sand, pebbles and small rocks, with a little greenery. Different stones represented specific elements of the natural landscape; mountains, seashores, even lakes.

Then gardeners discovered the art of growing miniature trees by cutting back and binding the roots of seedlings. These *bonsai* (grown in a bowl) have all the features of a tree growing in the great outdoors, but on the tiniest scale, and have become the most highly-prized feature of the Japanese miniature garden.

Bonsai are classified according to the shape into which they have been painstakingly trained, perhaps over hundreds of years. Those with upright, straight trunks suggest a forest setting, while sloping trunks are reminiscent of windswept cliffs, and dwarf pines with cascading branches speak of waterfalls.

The beauty of *bonsai* and miniature gardens is their size, allowing them to be moved wherever their picture of nature is needed to restore the spirit, perhaps in the living-room or inside the front door as a welcoming gesture to visitors.

Elizabeth Whiting

som, green summer foliage, autumnal colour and tracery of naked branches in winter.

In larger gardens, different trees may represent each season, with the Japanese maple (*Acer palmatum*) ablaze in autumn, and an ornamental crab apple (*Malus*) bearing its decorative fruit into winter.

The Japanese and Chinese place much less emphasis on colour than the West; plants are chosen more for the subtle tones and harmonies they add than for their brilliance. Foliage, therefore, is the main interest, with plants chosen for their leaf shape and texture. Moss is highly-prized, and bamboo, ferns and grasses are all prominent features.

Flowers add just a few accents of colour. Chrysanthemums have become as much an emblem of the Orient as the rose is of England, and, together with the azalea, iris, peony and lily, are chosen for their traditional symbolic associations with ideas of long life, blessedness, peace and everlasting happiness.

Basins and lanterns

Ornament is not essential to the oriental garden. Too much of it can destroy the tranquil sense of space, by overcrowding and distracting the eye from the subtleties of the 'natural' landscape. The water ba-

Ferns, with their subtle colours and unusual textures, can always find a place in an oriental garden. The delicate, tumbling fronds of Adiantum venustum (right) will soon cover a semi-shady bank.

In the oriental garden, gravel is used in many ways. Often, it is smoothed and rolled to represent water (left). Here, a path of large flat stepping stones enhances this effect. It also performs the function of a lawn, providing a base against which the delicate shapes and textures of other plants can be appreciated. It has two advantages over grass in this respect; it changes colour to reflect the weather and needs no mowing!

Coarser gravels give a different textural effect (right below), enhanced by contrast with the smoothness of water-rounded stones and pebbles, and make a fitting backdrop for sturdy, low-growing plants such as dwarf conifers.

Larger pebbles – though perhaps too hard on the feet to cover any large area – can make a delightful contrast to foliage plants with bold, undivided leaves, such as hostas (below).

even a basin. Trickling water brings life to the garden in its movement and musical sound, while the flat surface of a pond or basin provides scope for beautiful reflections. Whatever form it takes, a water feature must look as natural as possible, with ferns and aquatic plants mingling with the stones around the edge.

Seasonal cycles

Every aspect of the natural world is suggested in the oriental garden. The changing seasons may be represented in a flowering cherry (*Prunus*), with its delightful spring blos-

Harry Smith Collection

Eric Crichton

DRY GARDENS

The dry gardens of Japan are the ultimate expression of refined simplicity. In the temples of Zen Buddhism, these stark landscapes of rock and sand provided the perfect setting for undistracted meditation. For us they are an excellent source of decorative ideas for small, tranquil spots, and are especially useful in the context of a maintenance-free garden.

In the dry garden, water is suggested by a dry stream bed created from water-worn stones, or in expanses of sand from which rise boulders and rocks representing legendary islands symbolizing long life or joy eternal. Each weathered stone is selected with the greatest care and placed singly or with others in 'natural' asymmetrical groups. An illusion of greater depth is established by placing larger rocks in the foreground.

Often, moss is the only greenery, but small, carefully trimmed bushes such as box are sometimes used instead of boulders. There is no reason why a western equivalent should not be enlivened with just a handful of plants such as ferns, grasses and hostas, their foliage softening the mass of a boulder and contrasting well with the stark background.

The expanse of sand in temple gardens is meticuously raked into traditional patterns. Parallel lines represent waves, while ellipses and circles round stones are like water breaking on the rocks of an island.

These patterns need continuous attention to counter the disturbance of wind and rain, making them impractical for domestic gardens, unless on a very small scale. However, even a base of unraked gravel or pebbles offers lovely changes of texture and hue with sun and rain.

Harry Smith Collection

sin with its bamboo scoop and the stone lantern are, however, permanent features, introduced originally for religious purposes: the basin for cleansing the body and spirit; the lantern to represent the light of knowledge.

The water basin is usually of weathered stone but may be of another natural material – perhaps part of a fallen tree trunk, hollowed out. It is often raised on a flattened stone and enhanced by a very simple arrangement of rock and green foliage plants or moss. Again, the water may be represented by sand or fine gravel.

The idea of the lantern is not to rid the garden of the darkness but to enrich its mystery. It is most effective when placed to one side, perhaps in a shady spot against the foliage of trees and shrubs, whence it will cast intriguing, ever-changing shadows.

Architectural Plants

Grown for their bold shapes, architectural plants are often quite large, but just one or two can work wonders in the smallest garden.

Generally speaking, architectural plants are grown more for the striking beauty of their form than for colourful flowers. Many have stiff, upright leaves, suggesting a construction rather than a plant; others have leaves of large size or unusual shape.

Ideally, an architectural plant should also be evergreen, so that it is a permanent feature of the garden, not a seasonal event. The yucca is a classic example, with its tall sword-like leaves standing sentinel right through the year. Many architectural plants are tall, so that they stand out from the rest of the planting, but for the small garden there are plenty of more suitably sized but equally dramatic plants.

The average garden is designed on the general principles of the cottage garden, with borders packed as full of plants as possible. Usually, not much thought is given to their outline or leaf shape.

The result may be likened to an impressionist painting, full of drifts of colour but generally lacking in bold shapes, and often does not have much height to it. A garden designed on strictly architectural principles will contain far fewer plants, so that each one can be appreciated individually. It will be interesting all year round, but rather restrained – never a riot of colour.

Such plantings are generally most successful when carried out in small spaces that resemble outdoor rooms, furnished with paving, low walls, brick planters and tubs. They also have the virtue of being

S & O Mathews

labour saving, as the planting is confined to small, well-defined areas that are easy to look after.

For most gardeners, love of colour will prevent them from going all out for a truly architectural garden. However, there are two ways which architectural plants can be of great value in a more conventionally designed garden.

First, they can be used as accents – the horticultural equivalent of an exclamation mark – to give added interest to flower borders. Second, they can provide what our beloved roses, herbaceous perennials and gaily coloured annuals cannot – winter interest. Alternatively, you can grow

single architectural plants in handsome pots as a change from the usual annuals.

Familiar faces

Some of the best architectural plants are herbaceous perennials, once a familiar sight in gardens, that have been displaced by others with more showy flowers. Good examples are two prickly leaved plants, the globe thistle (*Echinops*) and sea holly (*Eryngium*).

Globe thistles are named for their perfectly ball-shaped flowerheads, in lovely shades of steel blue, standing singly on tall stems above a mass of large, deeply divided grey-green leaves. Sea holly has blue, teasel-like flowerheads,

Architectural plants are chosen for their dramatic outlines and sculptural shapes. This does not mean that they are all colourless. The flower heads of the long-stemmed kniphofia, for instance, are particularly warm and vibrant. This one (above) is K. rooperi.

The cardoon (Cynara cardunculus, right) is closely related to the artichoke. A native of the Mediterranean, where its leafstalks are eaten like celery, it needs protection from frosts, but given that produces handsome clumps of much-divided leaves with a grey-green flush (right) and large, thistle-like summer blooms.

TENDER PLANTS

Some of the best architectural plants are rather tender. Plant them in elegant containers which you can move to a shed or greenhouse before the frosts.

Plants in this category include:

● Century plants (*Agaves*) – strap-shaped leaves, sharp-pointed and spiny-edged, grey-green or variegated.

● Cabbage tree (*Cordyline australis*) – bunches of sword-shaped leaves on trunk-like stem. This one will survive outdoors in mild winters.

All plants in the Cordyline genus have good architectural qualities, but their use is restricted by a tendency to tenderness. C. australis, the New Zealand cabbage palm, is slow-growing, and makes a good container subject for a patio. All varieties produce a fountain of lance-shaped leaves; several, such as 'Torbay Red' (left) have unusual colours.

surrounded by a big ruff of spiny grey bracts. Both are as tough as they look, and will survive in poor soil, frost and even a drought.

A relative of the globe thistle (they are both knapweeds), the globe artichoke (*Cynara scolymus*), although mainly grown to eat, also makes a striking border plant. It has large, much-divided, greyish-blue foliage, and thistle-like blue flowers above the handsome green bracts, which are the part normally eaten.

Another old favourite, grown for its stately, column-shaped heads of yellow-green, long-lasting bracts is spurge (*Euphorbia*). This is another good plant for poor soils. The tall ones are *E. characias* (often evergreen) and *E. c. wulfenii*, both reaching 1.2m/4ft.

Building with colour

Some popular herbaceous perennials, grown for their beautiful blossoms, also qualify as architectural or accent plants because they flower on tall, upright stems. The outstanding

Globe thistles (Echinops spp.) are named for their ball-shaped flowerheads, carried on tall, slender stems. E. ritro (below) has, as an added attraction, deeply divided leaves that are noticeably downy on the underside.

short-lived and need staking, but are well worth the effort.

Another tall and stately plant is the strange-looking red-hot poker (*Kniphofia*). The sturdy spikes of tubular flowers rising as high as 1.8m/ 6ft from grassy foliage, are usually yellow, with hot red or orange tips. But, if these do not appeal, they can also be obtained in cooler cream, yellow and greenish yellow.

Good for shady beds are monkshood (*Aconitum* spp.), with tall spikes of helmet-shaped flowers, commonly violet-blue, and robust glossy leaves, and the biennial foxglove (*Digitalis* spp.), with tall spikes of large tubular flowers in many colours, attractively spotted inside.

Tropical look

Some of the most striking architectural plants are ones with stiff, swordlike, spiny leaves which give them an exotic, tropical look. The yucca family includes some of the hardiest and handsomest.

There are numerous varieties, but all form a dense clump of bayonet-like, shiny green or variegated leaves

example must be garden or Russell lupins, with their showy spikes in white, yellow, orange, red-purple and blue, raised above large leaves evenly divided into fingers. They flower early, but are not long-lived, and prefer lime-free soil.

Equally popular is the delphinium family, traditionally grown for its magnificent rich

Lupins are another good way of adding summer colour to an architectural design. The 'Russell Hybrids' (above) are particularly suitable, throwing their multi-coloured racemes up to 1.5m/5ft above a border.

blue flower spikes, though these can also be pink, mauve, yellow, red or white, often with a contrasting dark eye known as a 'bee'. The most suitable as accent plants are varieties of *D. elatum*, which grow up to 2.4m/8ft. Delphiniums are

---

SUMMER HOLIDAYS

Many houseplants have bold architectural foliage and will grow happily in the garden during the summer months. Suitable ones include:
- Aspidistra
- Desert cacti such as mammillarias and prickly pears.
- False castor oil plant (*Fatsia japonica*).
- Palms such as *Phoenix* (date palm), *Washingtonia* (Californian fan palm) or *Trachycarpus* (windmill palm).
- Spider plants
- Succulents such as aloes and crassula.

BRIGHT IDEAS

The sea hollies (Eryngium spp.) combine divided, well-coloured leaves with strong shapes and attractive, thistle-like flowers and bracts. E. giganteum (right), with its silver-grey stems, bluish flowers and shiny bracts, is a particularly fine example, but does not live as long as others in the genus, dying after flowering.

60cm-3m/2-10ft high, some razor sharp, others edged with curly white fibres. The spectacular spikes of large, creamy-white, bell-like flowers may take some time to appear, but should come annually thereafter if the plant is in full sun, not every seven years as sometimes alleged.

A similar, but slightly less hardy plant is New Zealand flax (*Phormium tenax*); protect it with mulch if it is left outdoors in winter. It may produce rusty red, tubular flowers, followed by curved, scimitar-like seed pods up to 10cm/4in long. The species has olive green leaves, and there are many variegated varieties, some in stunning solid shades of red and purple, others striped green and yellow.

Tall grass

Grass does not sound very architectural, but several tall, ornamental grasses make splendid architectural-style centrepieces for lawns or circular beds.

Perhaps the most popular is pampas grass (*Cortaderia selloana*). Its arching, grey-green, saw-toothed leaves grow up to 1.8m/6ft long, and are evergreen except in very cold districts. In late summer, the clump throws up huge

Derek Gould

Photos Horticultural

Pampas grass (Cortaderia selloana) has a delightful shape, with its clumps of arching leaves overtopped with a mass of billowy plumes. It makes a fine specimen plant year round, but is particularly valuable in the winter, when a dusting of frost or snow makes its flower heads even more imposing (above). Zebra grass (Miscanthus sinensis 'Zebrinus', right) is no less imposing, but, by contrast, is at its best in the summer, when its variegated leaves put on a spectacular show, and in autumn, when it produces flowers in the shape of loose panicles of white spikelets.

feathery plumes of creamy-white flowers on tall stout stalks, which sometimes last until the following spring.

Some of its varieties, such as 'Pumila', are smaller and more compact, better for a small garden. 'Rendatleri' has beautiful, purplish-silver plumes. Wear gloves when removing any dead leaves from the clump as they are razor-sharp.

Another tall, impressive-looking plant is silver grass (*Miscanthus* spp.). One of the most attractive species, zebra grass (*M. sinensis* 'Zebrinus'), has yellow bands across the narrow green leaves, and dainty plumes of silky white flowers flushed red or purple.

Some silver grasses grow up to 3m/10ft tall; zebra grass only reaches about 1.2m/4ft. They are herbaceous, but the dead foliage can be left on the plant to provide winter interest, and when cut back in spring the plants grow with astonishing speed.

Bamboos are a kind of giant

grass, with hollow woody stems. They make fine specimen plants, but need careful choice as some are very invasive, spreading widely by underground rhizomes, and some can also reach 6m/20ft high.

A good choice for the small garden is *Arundinaria (Sinarundinaria) murielae*, which forms clumps of arching yellow-green canes 2.1-3m/7-10ft tall, topped with dark green leaves, and is non-invasive. It is moderately hardy, but it needs to be protected from cold winds. Plant other bamboos in tubs to control the rhizomes, or sever them regularly with a spade.

Herbaceous plants with

Many varieties of spurge are rather small, but larger ones are good architectural plants. The stems of Euphorbia characias wulfenii (right), for instance, can reach 1.2m/4ft. It is a perennial with biennial stems; each bears densely-packed grey-green leaves one year, and masses of yellow-green blooms the following spring.

The finely divided, fresh green, outer fronds of the ostrich fern (Matteuccia struthiopteris, below) are sterile. Darker, fertile inner fronds appear in the summer.

S & O Mathews

Andrew Lawson

huge leaves are best planted alone, as a feature in a front garden, or to fill an odd corner, though they might find a place at the back of a large border.

Friendly giants

One such is ornamental rhubarb (*Rheum palmatum*), related to ordinary rhubarb but inedible. The great glossy leaves, deeply toothed, can span 90cm/3ft, and form massive clumps. Large spikes of small fluffy pink flowers up to 2.4m/8ft high are produced in early summer. This plant does best in full sun and moist soil.

An equally handsome moisture-loving plant, with umbrella-shaped leaves up to 30cm/1ft across, and creamy white flower plumes, is *Rodgersia podophylla*. The leaves start off bronze, turn green and finish up coppery.

Not so big, but striking in shape and much loved by painters and sculptors, are the leaves of bear's breeches (*Acanthus spinosus*). They are deeply, jaggedly cut, each division tipped with a spine (perhaps the name comes from the idea that only a bear could tolerate them next to the skin!)

ATTRACTING BIRDS

Several handsome architectural plants produce seed heads that will attract finches and other seed-eaters if left on the plant in winter. Best ones are:
- Sunflower – huge yellow daisy with central boss of seeds; hardy annual.
- Teasel – large oval prickly seed heads; hardy biennial.

and up to 40cm/16in long. The sturdy flower spikes are equally striking, consisting of white and purple tubular blooms protected by leafy spine-tipped bracts. The plant grows to about 1.2m/4ft high.

As they reproduce by spores, ferns do not flower, and their interest lies solely in their graceful fronds. They are ideal as architectural plants in wild or woodland gardens, where yuccas or pampas grass would look out of place, and are generally ultra-hardy, preferring a moist soil and shade.

Fascinating ferns

Although herbaceous ferns are interesting for most of the year, in spring they slowly unfurl from tightly coiled heads to reveal the full glory of the fresh green, multi-divided fronds. These are followed by fertile fronds, differently

S & O Mathews

Andrew Lawson

The yucca genus has many members. All have masses of long, sharp, lance-shaped, arching leaves and infrequent, but spectacular, shows of flowers. The only drawback is that some are on the tender side. Y. gloriosa 'Variegata' (above) is hardier than some, and well worth growing for its yellow-edged leaves and huge panicles of pendulous, creamy-white flowers.

The rhubarb genus is another with many spectacular members. Rheum palmatum (left) is typical, forming a spreading clump of massive, lobed leaves and panicles of tiny, off-white, early summer flowers.

shaped and coloured. Some turn bronze in autumn, and the old brown fronds remain attractive in winter.

There is a multitude of fern species, all subtly different. Good tall ones include the native British buckler fern (*Dryopteris*), with delicate, pale green arching fronds, and the ostrich or shuttlecock fern (*Matteuccia*). This is more upright, and named for the way the fronds resemble a vase full of ostrich feathers, which later surround a shuttlecock-shaped circle of shorter, darker, fertile fronds.

The shield fern (*Polystichum*) is less tall and more spreading, with very finely divided fronds growing from a distinctive brown midrib. Perhaps most handsome of all is the royal fern (*Osmunda*), that can grow to 1.8m/6ft tall. Its fertile fronds resemble dried flowers, and in autumn it turns a rich brown.

Summer Houses

Summer houses can be invaluable as a handy store for garden furniture, or as an extra room with a view. They also can make a useful winter retreat.

Stephen Dobson/Garden Picture Library

A summer house is the sensible solution for storing garden furniture, but it can also make a good place to sit when the weather is too damp or cold to be out in the garden.

It is somewhere handy for children to play and keep their toys, and it makes a good part-time office for anyone working from home.

Add some insulation and perhaps a small heater, and a summer house can even be used as a garden room, to overwinter plants such as pelargoniums and fuchsias that need to be kept frost-free in winter, or to protect tubs of perennial plants or shrubs during bad spells of weather.

Basic designs

Today's summer houses are invariably made from wood – usually cedarwood, deal or other softwood. Three basic designs are available. The first is a round- or octagonal-shaped summer house which is similar to a round greenhouse, but has a solid roof and glass above waist level round one half of the building. (These are easiest to fit into a very small garden, but are the most expensive to buy.)

The second design is a chalet-style summer house that has one part totally enclosed by timber walls and glass doors and windows in the front. There is a covered veranda so you can sit outside but still receive some shelter

---

BRIGHT IDEAS

WINTER HEAT

Make a summer house comfortable for winter use by installing a portable gas heater; no electrical supply is necessary.

Photos Horticultural

Photos Horticultural

from the roof.

The third looks similar to a garden shed, but instead of being constructed entirely of timber, it has opening glass windows in the top half of the door, front and part of the side panels to let plenty of light in. Though not so beautiful as a chalet-style summer house, this type is probably the best value, as it gives the greatest covered area for storage.

All types of wooden summer houses are available in a fair range of sizes. If you cannot find a make that you like and which fits the space you have available, you can always have your own design built by a local joiner. Ask for a quotation, it may not cost quite so much as you think.

What to look for

Send for as many brochures from different suppliers as possible, and compare the cost of similar models carefully, weighing up any minor differences in construction and quality to find the best value. When making your choice, read the small print carefully before signing anything.

Check to see that everything you need to complete the house is included in the price – roofing felt, glass, nuts and bolts, fittings and so on. Check too that corrosion resistant window- and door-fittings are supplied, and that the timber has been treated with preservative. Finally, look to see if the manufacturers offer a guarantee, and what is covered by it.

Siting

In a small garden, unfortunately, you do not always have the space to site a summer house in an ideal spot. Indeed, if you are planning to use it mainly for storing garden furniture, the choice of site is not especially important.

It is, however, a good idea to keep to a fairly open situation

ALTERNATIVE STRUCTURES

● Convert a wooden shed or brick outhouse by replacing the solid front and door with a new frame and substituting glass panels, either from floor to roof or from waist level up. If you are not a good DIY-er, get a local builder to do the job for you. Add decorative trellis-work and climbers to give a new look to an unattractive, old building.

● Wendy houses are like walk-in dolls' houses and are ideal for children to play and store their toys in. They are, however, probably too small for most normal garden furniture, and much better suited to part of the play area in a garden.

Bulldog Garden Buildings

A Wendy house (left) makes a charming addition to the children's play area and solves the problem of storing toys.

When planning the site of a summer house, try to position it in the garden area that gets the maximum amount of sunlight (below left).

Just as important as the site are the surroundings of the summer house (right). Here a careful blend of colourful plants and a raised bed provides visual interest for the occupants inside.

Glassed walls (below) give this summer house a view on all sides and a lovely airy atmosphere in which to relax.

– under trees, for instance, the lack of air movement and water droplets falling after rain can make the wood rot.

A sunny situation is obviously best for a summer house that is primarily for sitting in. If space limits you to a spot that does not get the sun all day round, consider what time of day you are most likely to want to use it.

If you are out at work all day, for instance, then the summer house will probably be used most in the evening, in which case choose a spot that receives evening sun. And where possible site the struc- ture so it looks out over the best view possible, so you enjoy your time sitting inside it.

Building

Summer houses are bought in sectional form, the same way as sheds. Manufacturers

Peter McHoy

BRIGHT IDEAS

GARDEN STORES

If you don't have enough room for a summer house, or you want to use it as a playroom or office in winter, use a garden store (such as a large weatherproof box whose top opens as a lid) to store furniture and other items during the winter months.

---

should provide full instructions. Check all parts are present when the 'kit' is delivered.

Garden buildings are not difficult to put up, though it is best to have several strong helpers available. (Alternatively, get a local builder to put it up for you if you prefer.)

First, prepare the site by levelling it, and firm soft soil by treading well down. Then mark the site out and lay foundations of brick or paving slabs on concrete to support the cross-sections under the floor of the house. These only need to be one brick or slab high, to provide a firm base and raise the floor section slightly above ground level. This allows air to circulate freely beneath, which, in turn, helps stop the wood rotting.

The floor section is laid first, then wall sections are bolted in place. The roof is put on last; this should be covered with roofing felt. You can finish off the inside of the building by tacking wall boards, plywood or chipboard sheets to the interior uprights – this not

only looks much better, but it also acts as insulation and a draught excluder.

Planting suggestions

Choose nicely scented climbers – climbing or rambling roses, jasmine and honeysuckles – to cover the roof and walls. Plant perfumed plants such as scented pelargoniums, night scented stocks, pinks and lavender in beds surrounding the summer house.

In a larger border, grow scented lilies, old-fashioned, flowering tobacco and roses. Summer houses also look good with windowboxes – plant these with hyacinths in spring, and trailing annuals such as petunias (which will appreciate the shelter, even though they are not scented), in summer.

It is a good idea to plant winter-scented plants such as wintersweet (*Chimonanthus fragrans*), winter heliotrope and *Viburnum fragrans* along the path to the summer house if you use it in the 'off season', as you will get some benefit *en route* to your retreat.

DON'T FORGET!

MAINTENANCE

Apply a finishing coat (of coloured water repellant) when the building is up. Then give an annual coat of preservative. Choose a colour the same as the original treatment, to protect against rotting – this will also maintain the colour of the wood.

Comfortable Garden Furniture

Outdoor furniture is an integral part of your garden and the decisions that you make on the type and style of furniture are as important as the decisions that you make about overall garden design and planting.

Relaxing in your garden is an important part of outdoor living, but unless it can be done in comfort much of the pleasure is lost. All too often, the selection and positioning of permanent chairs, benches and patio furniture is considered far too late in the planning of a garden.

The right view

An attractive bench positioned towards the end of a garden – either in a formal design framed by statuesque conifers in large pots, or in an informal setting, perhaps canopied by a rustic arch clothed in sprawling climbers – can become a strong visual element in the garden's design.

It also fulfils a practical function; with age, gardeners need staging posts where a moment's rest can be claimed! It is equally important that the view from benches and chairs is not obstructed.

Range of materials

The wide range of potential materials includes wood, a combination of canvas and wood, metal, plastic-covered metals, metal and canvas, stone and reconstituted stone, and finally, plastic and moulded glass-fibre.

Furniture made from these can be grouped into three types – tables and chairs for creating an outside eating area, usually on a patio; chairs, benches and deckchairs for comfortable relaxation, either on a patio or at various positions in a garden;

Ron Sutherland/Garden Picture Library

and furniture on which to sunbathe around a pool or on a sheltered patio.

Furniture must be in harmony with its surroundings. The key to this is to use items constructed of natural materials on surfaces that have a natural appearance. For example, wooden furniture is ideal on brick surfaces or grass, but as brightly-coloured paving slabs tend to dominate wood, then white, plastic furniture is preferable.

Wood

The natural colour and grain of wood ensures it becomes part of a garden and does not fight with all the other features for attention.

Harmony is the key word to remember when buying furniture for the garden, patio or verandah. Here a Mediterranean-style whitewashed wall and trellis (above) set off the elegant white table and matching seats to perfection.

BRICK SEATS

Purpose-built permanent seats are usually only practical in warm areas. Patios are prime candidates for built-in seats, especially if they can be integrated into a retaining wall. Slatted wooden tops – moveable or permanent – make the bricks more comfortable to sit on.

The tops of walls can also be converted into seats, but take care that it is not possible to fall off them backwards.

Harry Smith Collection

If the wood is painted white the situation is reversed and it immediately captures the eye, often to the detriment of other attractive features. However, even this can be used to advantage when trying to create, say, a bright, Mediterranean-style patio.

Oak furniture is expensive but long-lasting; it ages to a light, brittle shade that harmonizes well with mellow-toned brick surfaces and therefore seldom looks right on brightly-coloured patios.

Benches can be placed almost anywhere in a garden. They can be set into a circular patio wall (above) to provide a welcome resting place for the weary gardener. Or use old weathered bricks and a plank to make a seat with a difference (below), around which dwarf box has been trained.

Benches are ideal for positioning around a garden, as well as on a patio. Those made of oak or teak have long life-spans, while softwood types have a shorter life but can last for a reasonable number of years if they are regularly maintained and protected from rain and snow in winter. Benches are frequently sold in sections, ready for construction at home.

Softwood picnic tables with integral seats are popular and ideal for patios and lawns. Take care, however, that the table does not tip up when several people are sitting on one side only. Such tables are often better suited to be used by children than by adults.

Collapsible wooden stools and tables (that can be stored in sheds or lofts in winter) are ideal for patio use in summer. Many are easily made by do-it-yourself enthusiasts, but do ensure they are secure and will not collapse while in use, perhaps trapping fingers.

Deckchairs are still popular and have the virtue of adapting to all human shapes, being comfortable and folding flat for easy storage. The canvas seat can be easily renewed.

Collapsible chairs resembling those used by directors on film sets are made of a wooden frame with a canvas seat and back. They are adaptable and often better than deckchairs for people who cannot bend down easily.

Metal

Metal furniture is durable and versatile. Traditional wrought-iron tables, chairs and benches have a rustic charm that harmonizes with

David Squire

BRIGHT IDEAS

SUN UMBRELLAS

Large, brightly-coloured umbrellas are very welcome in summer. Most are available to go with patio tables. The supporting pole passes through the table and is anchored in a container filled with water or sand.

If you live in an area where the atmosphere is polluted, periodically wash the cover. And always collapse the shade at night and when the umbrella is not in use.

informal settings while modern furniture with formal outlines – perhaps painted white – is ideal for positioning on brightly-surfaced patios. Corrosion is the main disadvantage of furniture made of ferrous metal, but regular painting should prevent this from happening.

Metal also invariably creates a hard, unyielding surface, which is usually cold although in summer it sometimes becomes startlingly hot. Moveable cushions are the answer to this problem.

Lightweight, aluminium-framed collapsible chairs with attractive canvas seats are comfortable and usually available with adjustable back supports. Most are fitted with arm rests. Although aluminium is non-ferrous and therefore does not rust when wet, the canvas

On a patio, wicker furniture has the advantage of being light and easy to move (above). But take care to protect it from the weather.

Nothing beats a solid wooden table and chairs (below) for blending in with the garden's natural features. Oak and teak are the most durable woods, but softwood can be used for a number of years if it is properly treated with preservative.

must not be allowed to become wet. Their light weight allows them to be stored away in winter. Infirm and old people find them easy to handle.

Plastic-covered metal furniture is strong and non-rusting, with the advantage that it can be wiped clean after children have spilled drinks or food.

Plastic

Plastic has revolutionized garden furniture. Moulded tables and chairs are widely available, usually in white, often in sets, and at prices that make them attractive. The chairs are usually stackable and easily stored in winter.

Designs of chairs are varied, usually providing a comfortable sitting position with good lumbar support, especially those with arms and high backs. Also, they can be left outside throughout summer, needing only a wipe with a cloth after a rain shower.

Chairs at the upper end of the price range are usually available with detachable, padded covers that make sitting easier over a long period.

Bramley Garden Furniture, Braintree

cement – to fix the top securely to the supports.

Large foliaged shrubs positioned behind a stone seat, as well as sprawling ground-cover plants, will help to unify it with the surroundings.

Make your own seats

Part of the fun of gardening is to create something not seen often in other gardens, and distinctive seats are certainly a possibility.

The simplest type of bench is a strong plank, 1.2-1.8m/4-6ft long, 25-38cm/10-15in wide and about 5cm/2in thick, secured to two supports about 45cm/18in high. The 'legs' could be two 13-18cm/5-7in thick logs, 75cm-1m/2½-3ft long that are firmly buried in the ground.

The plank is then nailed to them – but first drill holes in the plank so that it is not split by large nails.

A slightly more ambitious seat is a wooden plank integrated into a background of dwarf box (*Buxus sempervirens* 'Suffruticosa'), a small-leaved evergreen.

First construct supports from old, well-weathered bricks cemented together.

Oval and round tables are most commonly seen, often with a hole in the centre so that a sun umbrella can be fitted to provide much needed shade in very hot weather.

Collapsible chairs formed of rigid, reinforced plastic frames are widely available. They can be easily stored in winter. To make them more comfortable, padded seats and back covers can be purchased.

Stone

Stone seats are a permanent feature and therefore must be carefully integrated with the rest of the garden. They should not be obtrusive, yet if the supports are attractively sculptured – perhaps in the form of lions or other animals – these should not be hidden.

Additionally, such a seat needs a position offering good views of the garden.

Real stone is invariably expensive, but many companies producing statues and other garden ornaments from reconstituted stone also make attractive rectangular slabs that can be used for creating seats when they are placed on firm supports.

Use a weak mortar mix – eight parts of sand to one of

Traditional-style wrought-iron furniture (above) looks particularly charming.

A sundial (below) or a statue can become a focal point on an uncanopied patio with built-in seating.

Derek Gould

Place the plank on top and set it into the mortar. The dwarf box can then be trained and clipped around it.

Care of furniture

To ensure the maximum length of life, yearly maintenance and protection during winter is essential, especially for wooden furniture. Where possible, place garden furniture under cover when the weather deteriorates.

Rain, snow and freezing temperatures damage wood and by spring renovation is needed. Of course, hot summer sun can be just as damaging, drying the surface and warping thin, unseasoned wood. Use first coarse, then fine

Bird baths encourage wildlife and add character to a garden particularly when nestling amid a charming display of roses (above).

Sink into the comfort of a chair or chaise longue (below). Here, durable plastic furniture makes for affordable luxury.

sandpaper to prepare the surface, then apply several coats of varnish, allowing each coat to dry thoroughly before applying the next. Teak furniture is maintained by cleaning and coating with teak oil.

If left outside in autumn, stand wooden benches and tables on bricks to prevent them resting in water. Wrap the piece of furniture in polythene sheeting, tying it firmly to the legs.

Move all wooden furniture from lawns as if it remains there in winter it encourages the legs to rot. Always put deckchairs under cover.

Check metal furniture for rust; if any is found, remove with sandpaper, then paint.

Stone and reconstituted stone seats usually need smartening up in spring. Wash with soapy water, gently rubbing with a soft brush. Then rinse thoroughly with clean water.

S & O Mathews

'Le Chateau' range: Besco Baron, Rochdale

Choosing Garden Ornaments

Decorative ornaments – whether they are stone urns, sea-sculpted driftwood or humble gnomes – can add interest, surprise and humour to any garden.

The words 'garden ornaments' mean different things to different people. For some they mean statues, urns and fountains. For others, the more homely vision of gnomes and wishing wells comes to mind. Of course, both fall into the category of garden ornaments, but this does not mean that you must stick rigidly to one or the other. An imposing urn does not necessarily rule out the possibility of having a garden gnome. It is all a matter of personal taste.

Strictly speaking, an ornament should serve no useful purpose other than that of decoration. In reality, of course, ornaments often turn out be useful as well as decorative. Sundials and birdbaths, for instance, are both ornamental and functional.

Personal style

Most people enjoy developing their own taste and style and expressing it in their clothes and in their homes. When you paint and decorate your house, it is the choice of colours, pictures and ornaments that transforms it from just any house into a home stamped with your personal style.

This same process of reflecting your personality and creativity in your surroundings may be carried beyond the four walls of your home and into your garden. Colours, textures and ornaments can turn your patch of ground into an exciting extension of your home.

A dark background of evergreens sets this statue (right) off perfectly while complementing its classical simplicity and elegance.

Eric Crichton

Eric Crichton

Wind chimes, whether shop-bought (above) or home-made from shells and small pieces of polished driftwood, can add a new dimension to your enjoyment of your garden.

A sundial (below) makes a useful as well as a decorative ornament in the garden. Choose between genuine antiques, copies and more modern designs.

To avoid making costly mistakes, you will need to take time and care in considering what you want from your garden. Will it be formal or informal? Do you want it to have one complete overall 'look', or do you want to create different moods in different areas?

The decisions you make at this early stage will influence your choice of ornaments. Whatever you decide, planning and a bit of window shopping will save time, energy and money in the long term. Having some kind of decorating scheme in mind also enables you to see things around you with a fresh eye. Garden ornaments do not have to be bought in a garden centre. What was once a piece of junk or a 'find' on a beach can become an ornament – and at little or no cost.

Nature provides a huge array of lovely things that can be used to enhance your garden for free. When you go to the seaside, keep a weather eye open for interesting pieces of driftwood. Exposure to sea, sand and waves over a long period can produce some wonderful shapes and textures. These finds make lovely natural sculptures for your garden and can either stand alone or be incorporated into all sorts of arrangements of rocks, shells and stones.

Beach finds
Large, flattish shells such as scallops can be used as edging for a bed or path in a cottage or informal garden. A dazzling variation is to paint them in bright, waterproof colours. This is particularly handy in a shady border which needs cheering up. A more subtle approach is to select natural shades that match some of the plants or act as a contrast.

Smaller shells may be scattered around plants in window boxes and pots as a more decorative alternative to gravel or bare soil. Particularly exquisite shells and pebbles

from sun-kissed holidays can beautify water features such as ponds and fountains.

Beaches often provide fragments of coloured glass and pottery, worn smooth by the waves. These make lovely mobiles to hang from tree branches, brackets or pergolas. Shells and small pieces of polished driftwood can be used in this way, too. If you select your materials with care, they can act as wind chimes, making a pleasant tinkling sound as the breeze blows.

Woodland look
Logs and tree stumps can all play a part in decorating your garden. A group of different-sized logs can make wonderful stands for flower pots, for example. Fill them with a selection of dwarf spring bulbs, primroses and various forms of ivy for a woodland look. Such an arrangement is particularly pleasing on a flight of steps or a patio. A similar display will soften a gravel path and the combination of varying heights and textures is especially attractive.

Harry Smith Collection

Harry Smith Collection

The type of ornament you choose should complement the style of your garden. This rustic hand pump and stone trough (left) are perfectly suited to this charming cottage garden but would look out of place in more formal surroundings.

The stylized bird bath (below left), would fit happily into either a formal or more informal setting.

An old tree stump need not be an eyesore (below). Use it as a pot stand for a constantly changing display or hollow it out, add some compost, and plant directly into it.

Rustic containers of various sizes may be made from logs simply by hollowing out the centre and drilling drainage holes. Add plenty of crocks for drainage and plant in the usual way. If used lengthways they make fine window boxes as long as you cut a slice from the base of each log to ensure it does not wobble, but sits firmly on the window sill. You can buy such boxes, but it is considerably cheaper to make your own.

Tree stumps left in a bed or on a lawn need not be an eyesore – they can be used as pot stands. Another attractive idea is to cover the top surface with small gravel and bed a shallow container into it. Make up a mixture of sharp sand and compost and surround the container with it, without quite reaching the edges of the stump. Cover the mixture with an arrangement of nicely shaped stones and

COPY CAT

Painted tins provide unusual ornaments and make useful containers. Take inspiration from a variety of design sources.

● Bargeware from canal boats features roses and castles which look stunning on a dark background.

● The dazzling motifs and colours of the funfair are another source of ideas.

● The ancient Greeks and Celts knew a thing or two about decoration and some of their patterns are remarkably simple when you take a close look.

● The 1930s sunset motifs used on stained glass, radios and garden gates can be very effective and are simple to copy.

● Any well-stocked library should have good pattern references, or take a look around your own home and copy designs from fabrics or china.

After all the 'serious' groundwork is done, remember your garden is something to enjoy and have fun with, so let your garden ornaments be as frivolous as you like. In this garden (left), a playful cat brings a touch of humour as it climbs down the wall in search of imaginary prey.

The classic stone urn (right) is always popular and can find a place in any garden. Its strong shape needs no embellishment: filling it with plants would only spoil the effect. Its only drawback is that it will not be cheap to buy.

Another ornament in the form of an animal. This innocent-looking white kitten (below left) gazes out from a sea of snowdrops. 'Fun' ornaments like this are best suited to a natural, informal garden.

pebbles and continue to the very edge of your platform. Plant a few creeping rock plants, dwarf bulbs and perhaps some variegated ivy near the edge. Fill the container with water and you have a very pretty bird bath.

Never throw anything away until you are sure it cannot become a garden ornament. Yesterday's junk could turn out to be today's treasure. Tins of various sizes that once held paint or oil may be painted in bright colours and used as plant pots for the patio. An outdoor staircase can be transformed by groups of containers jostling for space on each step. Geraniums do well in them and give your garden a Mediterranean look. Trailing plants give the impression of a floral cascade and ferns and other foliage plants add a lushness to shaded areas. Remember to make drainage holes in the base of tins and provide plenty of crocks.

Old chimney pots make great plant stands and kettles, teapots, casserole dishes and saucepans can also make good containers. Old wheelbarrows and metal buckets can be painted with cheerful designs and filled with complementary summer bedding. Again, always put plenty of crocks at the bottom before planting to provide drainage.

Shop around

You may already have a plan for your garden and a firm idea of what ornaments you wish to buy. Shop around as prices vary from place to place. Sometimes it is possible to pick up slightly damaged goods at greatly reduced prices, and small cracks or chips can easily be disguised with foliage. Time spent browsing in garden centres, junk shops and at jumble sales is never wasted. It can also be a great deal of fun.

If you would like your

DARK CORNERS

BRIGHT IDEAS

Q There is a dark area in our garden formed by the garage and a tall brick wall. How can I make it more interesting or even turn it into a feature?

A Fixing a large mirror to the rear wall and surrounding it with trellis to soften its edges will give a feeling of space and light. Check that the backing is suitable for outdoor use when buying. Grow climbers up the trellis and add an unusual ornament positioned so that it is reflected in the mirror.

statue, urn or trough to weather nicely and be covered with moss and lichens as it ages, you must choose carefully. Such plants will not 'take' on straight concrete but concrete ornaments can be treated with a preparation which enables moss to grow on them. Another option is to buy ornaments made of an aggregate of pulverized stone, sand and cement. Of course, real stone ornaments will age beautifully but they are very expensive.

Love at first sight

Sometimes it is love at first sight – you spot an ornament you must have at any price, and all ideas of careful planning fly out of the window. Never mind, it is always possible to work your garden design around an ornament. It may even prove to be the inspiration you need.

A classical urn or statue on a plinth is perfect for a formal setting with the ornament as a focal point. Alternatively, it may turn a leafy, overgrown area into a secret place, with a touch of faded splendour about it. Swathe the figure or urn with dark ivy to enhance this

The traditional brightly coloured garden gnome (above) invariably acts as a focal point, rather than blending naturally into its setting. Wherever it is placed, it will create a lighthearted cheerful atmosphere.

Stone lions, like this handsome specimen (right), are traditional garden ornaments. They look especially good when used to flank a doorway or entrance in a formal garden.

Eric Crichton

impression. Move it around until you are sure you have found the best place for it.

A stone toad, gnome or other small figure peeping out from beneath a hedge or among the flowers can add warmth and humour to a rather dull area. A stone cat can gaze down from a tree or wall top if securely placed, or peer through the blossoms of clematis grown along walls or over trees.

Animal magic

Lions or urns can look wonderfully imposing when flanking a patio or steps. A fawn or a deer in the dappled sunlight of a wooded area conjures up visions of peaceful glades. Stone foxes and badgers peering through an undergrowth of wild flowers give a feel of the real countryside.

An inventive and imaginative use of ornaments can turn your garden into a wonderland of interest, surprise and humour. A simple statue or a cluster of bright tins in the right setting will transform the dullest corner. Best of all, creating a stunning impression need not lead to financial ruin – it can often be achieved on a shoestring.

Eric Crichton

Children's Play Areas

Most children love to play in the open air. With care and imagination, a gardener can create a soft and stimulating environment for them to grow up in.

The list of things to be considered when you are planning your garden can be daunting. Which plants thrive in shade and which flourish in full sun? Where should you put the shed? What about a rock garden, a water feature, ornaments, winter colour and summer scents? How big will that tree or shrub grow, and is there room?

Browsing through books and gardening magazines can leave you both excited and thoroughly confused as to where to begin. You may be itching to get started as you brighten the winter months by poring over catalogues, but before you send off a flurry of orders, pause and have a quiet think about what you want.

The very first question you should ask yourself has nothing to do with plants, ponds and sheds. Who is going to use your garden and what are their needs?

It is a well known fact that most accidents occur in the home. With this in mind, most people are quite careful when decorating and furnishing their houses. The interests of the family members are taken into consideration when plans are made. The same care can and should be taken when planning your garden.

A place to play

Young children need safe play areas both in and out of the house. Even the very young get older and their interests change, so plans should be flexible and allow for this

natural movement from sand pit to ball games.

How you plan your garden depends a lot on how big it is. Large gardens can accommodate an area set aside for children's play, but bear in mind that children will wander, so the rest of the garden must be safe and durable too.

Smaller gardens will need to be planned with the recreational and safety needs of

everyone in mind. Thoughtful planning makes it possible to create a garden that is inviting both as a playground for your children and a peaceful haven for adults.

Gardens can be hazardous places. The most obvious dangers are chemicals and tools. These must be stored in a child-proof place. A garden shed with a sturdy lock is one solution. However, space may

An area set aside for children's play need not stick out like a sore thumb. The use of such common garden-centre products as rustic poles, log rolls and pulverized bark in creating a play area (above) enables it to be drawn into the overall garden scheme.

Greenhouses are full of sights and scents to stimulate young minds, so all chemicals and other hazardous materials should be stored beyond the reach of inquisitive fingers (left).

All children enjoy a place of their own in the garden, whether it is a special miniature house (below) or converted shed.

Pippa Johnson/Life File

Nicola Sutton/Life File

Marshall Cavendish

If you have a tree large enough, a wooden house in its branches (left) is an ideal retreat for older children.

be a problem. Sheds the size of a cupboard are available and can be tucked away quite neatly in a little-used corner.

Playing house

A small garden may not have room for both a shed and a play house. Play houses attract children of all ages, from the very young right through to the teenager who wants to entertain a few friends.

With a bit of forethought and some basic D I Y skills, safe storage can be incorporated in a play house. Chemicals and smaller tools can be kept in a locked chest which doubles as a window seat or bench. Larger tools can be locked away in an upright cupboard disguised, with a little paint and imagination, as a fireplace or kitchen range. It is important to make sure that any windows are made with safety glass. Later, when the children are grown, the play house can revert to a shed or be made into a summer house.

Climbing things is not only fun but is also a necessary part of a child's development. To save wear and tear on trees, fences and walls, provide a climbing frame.

One idea is to construct a wooden frame in the shape of

AN OUTDOOR CLASSROOM

There is no doubt that children can be hard on gardens. Rough games can ruin grass and borders alike. However, you can teach your children to respect the natural world and your garden makes a perfect classroom, if you show them it's fun.

Allow your children to 'help' with the gardening from a very early age. Discuss what you are doing and point out things of interest. Explain the dangers too.

Help your off-spring to make their very own garden and supply quick growing and colourful plants and seeds for rapid results.

Make your garden attractive to wildlife so that your children can discover interesting facts about birds, insects and pond-life, safely.

Help your children to keep a record of gardening events such as planting or visits from birds or butterflies.

Not only will such lessons help your children to respect your precious plants, but they will be a very valuable addition to their general education as well.

an Indian's teepee. The frame can then be made to double as a tent by simply throwing rugs or old blankets over it. Many imaginative games can be played in and around a tent. When your children outgrow it, it need not be a useless eyesore. Climbers such as clematis, honeysuckle or rambling roses will quickly turn it into a beautiful feature.

Water features

Water is always a magical element in a garden, attracting useful wildlife. A quiet, reflective pool or the soothing tinkle of a waterfall or fountain can be very restful, even therapeutic, in a stressful world.

It is possible, however, for a small child to drown in very shallow water. It is essential, therefore, that if you plan to make a pond it should be placed where you can easily keep an eye on it. Never allow a toddler unsupervised access to the pond. Perhaps the safest solution to this problem is not to have a pond at all until your children are old enough to be aware of the danger.

If you move into a house that has a pond already, then you must make it safe. A decorative fence around it is one option; draining it and turning

it into a sand pit is another. You can always reclaim it when your children are older.

Lawns

Many people feel that a garden is not a proper garden unless there is an area of lawn somewhere. The ideal, of course, is the wonderful smooth grass seen in illustrations of stately 'English' gardens. Lovely

though they are, such lawns were never meant to withstand the rough and tumble of family life. A little gentle bowls or croquet perhaps, but not the rugged attentions of your children and their friends. The secret is to pick your seed or turf with care.

There are many types of grass, but only a small proportion are suitable for lawns. No

Children like to 'help' in the garden (above). Encourage them by setting aside a small area for them to grow easy and colourful plants such as sunflowers. Most, though, prefer to play; if you have the space, a steel climbing frame (below) will give hours of fun and exercise.

single variety makes a good lawn on its own; it has to be blended with other kinds. The blending of these grass seeds is a highly skilled process which is developing all the time to produce mixtures suitable for a whole host of uses.

In order to make a lawn that can stand up to energetic play, you need a blend that has plenty of perennial ryegrasses in the mixture. These have been refined to produce fine-leaved, dwarf grasses that will tolerate the constant thunder of small feet day after day.

If you decide to buy turf instead of seed, your choice is more limited. It can be difficult to find out what seed mixture was used to produce the turf, so its durability cannot necessarily be assured. Turf is more expensive than seed, too, and poor quality turf may include unwanted weeds, pests and diseases.

Despite the drawbacks, turf does have the advantage of supplying an almost instant lawn. This can prove very useful if you have an urgent need for a play area that is kinder to knees than gravel or concrete.

Ponds and pools, especially when filled with fish, attract children like a magnet (right). They are however, dangerous places for small people. A low retaining wall as pictured here is not sufficient; a chest-high paling fence is needed to stop them tumbling in.

David Squire

PROJECT

BLENDING IN A PLAY AREA

The decision whether to set aside a specific area for play depends partly on the size of your garden. A small one would just not have the room.

Even if you have a huge garden, very young children should play close to the house for safety reasons. It is important, therefore, that this space should be pleasing to the eye.

Where possible, try to use natural materials for play equipment such as climbing frames. A home-made wooden structure can later become an arch or an interesting frame for climbers to scramble over.

You could incorporate a climbing area at one end of a pergola. This would make it blend in beautifully with the garden. To begin with, just plant climbers over part of

Michael Shoebridge

the structure and plant the rest when your children have outgrown climbing.

Use bark chippings in the play area to soften both landing and the contours. Spread it in an attractive shape and carry it through to a border or a path to give the impression of play area and

garden flowing into one another.

You could use the same bark as mulch for trees and shrubs in another area of the garden. This will help the play space to blend in by picking up the colour and texture elsewhere in the garden.

If you are lucky and have a garden large enough to set aside a space devoted to swings, slides and climbing frames, then it is best to provide a soft landing. Grass may put an end to skinned knees but a sun-baked lawn is still pretty hard. A better material for such an area is bark.

Hard-wearing pulverized bark, sold by garden centres for mulching, is particularly suitable for surfacing a play area. It has a pleasing, decorative appearance and gives a springy surface on which to land. Be fairly generous. Lay it on thickly and extend it for a

Childish imaginations can transform an elaborate climbing frame into a boat, a house, a bridge or a fort. Whatever the game, tumbles are likely, and a carpet of bark chippings will prevent serious injuries (right).

Small children tend to lack patience, and are not natural gardeners. However, if they are given a small area of their own where they can experiment (below), they can learn the basic skills in helping plants to grow.

Lillian Cowling/Life File

distance around the play equipment. It can always be recycled to mulch around shrubs and trees when the equipment is dismantled or put to other uses.

You can never protect your children against all possible

accidents. It is in the nature of children to explore their environment and test the limit of their abilities. They will try to climb a little higher or jump from greater heights. These voyages of discovery may be heart-stopping for you but they are essential to a developing child. A garden can, with imagination and planning, provide both a safe place to play and a wonderland of exploration into the joys of the natural world.

Harry Smith

Edging a Bed

Stylish edgings of dwarf plants or of hard materials, such as paving stones, logs or seashells, will greatly enhance the character of your borders.

Eric Crichton

Edgings for flower beds were at the peak of their popularity in Victorian times. Symmetrical beds of annuals with simple geometric designs were always finished off with formal edgings.

The technique also suits other, less formal, styles of garden. Rows of scallop shells, for instance, were often seen edging beds in romantic, ram-

bling Victorian cottage gardens. Today, logs are still popular for bordering paths in wild or woodland borders.

Modern gardens often contain several very different 'theme' beds. Whatever beds or other features you have, a carefully chosen edging will provide the finishing touch that brings out their character and individuality.

Flower beds of annuals, in the Victorian style, are back in fashion. Carpet bedding, for example, is catching on fast. Here a carpet-like pattern is created in a formal round or square bed, usually with low-growing flowers that simulate the look of a carpet. Sometimes beds have taller plants towards the centre to raise the pattern and make it

A form of basic edging to a bed is provided by a path, whether it be of gravel, as here, or of brick, paving slabs or tarmac. It is enhanced, though, by a firm edging of bricks, logs, rocks or other hard material. The planting itself, with tall plants at the back, is edged with low-growing petunias and pansies.

easier to view on a flat site.

Either way, a formal edging of very low-growing plants, to separate the bed from the surrounding lawn, is essential to the success of the scheme.

Alyssum is always a popular choice, but any neatly shaped, low-growing annuals, such as lobelia, ageratum, French marigolds or dwarf candytuft, could be used.

In autumn, remove the summer bedding and replace it with traditional spring-flowering wallflowers and/or bulbs. This springtime bed will look good with an edging of polyanthus or primroses.

Herbaceous border

This type of border is traditionally edged with hard materials, rather than low plants. Long, straight herbaceous borders often have formal hard edgings, but it is rare to see a modern island bed treated in this way. It is certainly worth trying, though, for the workload it can save you.

The border can be edged with metal or with real or synthetic stone edging strips sunk

EDGING A SCREE BED

For their rock plants most people have a scree bed, with a low retaining wall outlining its shape. Since this wall is the edging to the bed, it is important to keep it in character with the plants.

Stone must be the first choice. Second-hand York stone walling blocks are sometimes available in builder's merchants. Manufacturers now produce reconstituted stone walling and even blocks that look like natural dry-stone walling.

To complete the effect, top dress the finished bed after planting with stone chippings that match the stone edging.

GARDEN NOTES

GOOD PLANTS FOR EDGING

Plant	Colour	Height	Comments
Ageratum	Pink, white, blue	15-20cm/6-8in	Half hardy annual
Alyssum	Pink, white, mauve, purple	7.5-10cm/3-4in	Hardy annual
Anagalis	True blue	15-23cm/6-9in	Treat as a half hardy annual
Candytuft (*Iberis umbellata*)	Pink, white, lilac, carmine	23cm/9in	Hardy annual
Double daisy (*Bellis perennis*)	Pink, white, carmine	10-15cm/4-6in	Hardy biennial
Edging box (*Buxus sempervirens* 'Suffruticosa')	Dark evergreen shrub	clip to 10-20cm/4-8in	Formal edging for herb or knot gardens
French marigold (*Tagetes patula*)	Orange, yellow, mahogany	15cm/6in	Half hardy annual
Lavender 'Munstead Dwarf'	Mauve-flowered evergreen shrub	30cm/12in	Formal edging for cottage or knot gardens; stands regular clipping
Polyanthus (*Primula* hybrids)	Most colours	15-25cm/6-10in	Treat as a hardy biennial
Primrose (*Primula vulgaris*)	Most colours	7.5-15cm/3-6in	Hardy perennial but can be treated as biennial
Rosemary (*Rosmarinus officinalis* 'Miss Jessopp's Upright')	Blue-flowered evergreen shrub	1m/3ft	Stands tight clipping if done regularly
Snow-in-summer (*Cerastium tomentosum*)	White	15cm/6in	Invasive perennial

Derek Gould

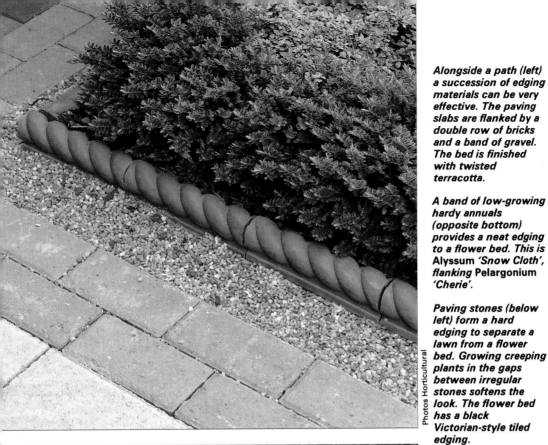

Photos Horticultural

Alongside a path (left) a succession of edging materials can be very effective. The paving slabs are flanked by a double row of bricks and a band of gravel. The bed is finished with twisted terracotta.

A band of low-growing hardy annuals (opposite bottom) provides a neat edging to a flower bed. This is Alyssum 'Snow Cloth', flanking Pelargonium 'Cherie'.

Paving stones (below left) form a hard edging to separate a lawn from a flower bed. Growing creeping plants in the gaps between irregular stones softens the look. The flower bed has a black Victorian-style tiled edging.

A raised bed (below) can be edged by a variety of hard materials. Here a 'fence' of halved logs is complemented by a path of bark chips.

WATER FEATURE

Ponds of pre-formed glass fibre or those lined with polythene or butyl rubber need something to merge the raw edge into the surrounding garden.

An edging of flat paving slabs does just that, and also provides a level non-slip surface from which to watch pond life. For a formal pond, regularly shaped pre-cast slabs laid in a continuous row round the edge are ideal.

In an informal setting, an irregular edging of differently sized natural or synthetic stone slabs looks more in keeping. More informally still, you could plant waterside plants thickly so as to overhang the edge of a truly wild pond. Leave just a hint of an edging with strategically placed stepping stones at the water's edge.

Bright Ideas

Andrew Lawson

Eric Crichton

in along the front of the bed. These should stand out about 5-7cm/2-3in above the edge of the lawn. You can now buy reproduction Victorian edgers with an attractive twist pattern to the top.

Any of these will provide a firm edge to the lawn, making it less likely to give way if someone stands on it to look at the flowers. They also prevent grass from growing into the bed, keeping a clean, sharp edge to the lawn.

These hard materials make it easy to tidy the edge of the grass with a nylon-line trimmer, since they provide a hard surface to trim against without the risk of damaging the plants in the bed.

Another useful idea for edging a border is a row of paving slabs right along the front of the bed. This provides a firm, dry path from which you can weed, plant or hoe.

Perennials that overhang the front of the bed will spill out over the path, not the grass. So, when you tidy away old stems and foliage in autumn, your lawn will be perfect, unmarked by the usual semicircular yellow or brown patches of dead grass.

Cottage garden border

Old fashioned cottage gardens frequently had a single row of cockle shells edging the path to the front door. Behind the shells were several rows of different flowering plants, graduating in height.

At the front were short double daisies (*Bellis perennis*) or fair-maids-of-France (*Saxifraga granulata*), while at the back were tall crown imperials, lavender, pinks, gladioli or cottage tulips. Behind this formal edging was the traditional random mixture of flowers, fruit trees and bushes.

The same sort of multi-layer edging adds charm to a modern cottage garden corner. Scallop shells may be obtained in quantity from fishmongers or restaurants. Alternatively, use oyster or mussel shells. Or you can cement cockle shells picked up at the beach to ordinary cement or stone edgers.

Authentic cottage garden edging plants are still readily available. Modern cottage gardeners may also use aubrieta, houseleeks, snow-in-summer (which tends to be invasive), alyssum or even chives.

A woodland or shady border

A very natural effect can be created from short lengths of log laid in a row to outline the shape of a path or the curve of a woodland bed.

This looks even better if you continue the theme by using a gnarled tree stump or a fallen trunk as features within the bed. They can be half hidden by woodland plants and shade lovers, such as ferns, foxgloves, silver birch trees and rhododendrons.

In a less wild setting a neater edging can be created

Photos Horticultural

Gillian Beckett

Eric Crichton

KNOT GARDEN

GARDEN NOTES

The knot garden is another old fashioned, formal garden style which is making a come-back. The beds are laid out in a complicated pattern, edged with a miniature hedge clipped to a height of 10-15cm/4-6in. The shapes are filled in with annuals, and gravel paths run between the beds.

Knot gardens are best planted close to the house. The patterns and the contrasts in colours and textures can then be viewed from above.

The traditional edging for knot gardens was dwarf box, but this is very slow growing. Dwarf lavender is often used instead, or you could even use an upright form of rosemary, which can be kept clipped into shape.

by using short pieces of treated timber wired together fence-style. These are available ready-made at garden centres, or you could easily make up your own.

They look particularly good used as a low retaining 'wall' in a shady border, partially hidden by hostas, brunnera, *Geranium phaeum* and Solomon's seal.

As herb gardens are mainly green with relatively few flowers, it is a good idea to include plenty of hard materials to offset the foliage. Brick or gravel paths and a sundial or birdbath provide a good contrast in texture.

Herb garden

A neat edging of old red bricks or small, square terracotta floor tiles, laid flat along the side of a gravel path, picks out the shape of the garden.

This idea can be taken one step further if you make a low retaining wall by setting on edge old red bricks or large flooring or roofing tiles — wavy pantiles are ideal. The unusual texture of clay land drainage pipes, standing on end in a row, can be very effective as an edging.

Add a 15cm/6in band of gravel to separate the edge of the bed from the grass, unless there is already a gravel path alongside it. A metal strip along the turf will stop gravel getting on the lawn.

Alternate clumps of white alyssum and purple lobelia (above left) form a distinct edging to a multi-coloured flower bed.

Tiles (above right) or bricks form a neat break between a lawn and a bed.

Pathways of brick (left) divide beds of herbs. The whole is enclosed by a rectangle of paving slabs with stone birdbaths and a broad band of gravel.

The intricate patterns of a knot garden are formed by low, well clipped hedges (right). The spaces between may be planted up or, as here, filled with gravel.

Derek Gould

Garden Lighting

If you think your day in the garden ends when dusk falls, let us throw a little light on the delights of the evening garden.

Garden lights can transform your garden at the flick of a switch. You will see it in a new light, view your plants in a fresh way, and discover a quietly different garden after dark.

Garden lighting does not have to be restricted to unimaginative floodlights. Instead you can explore the possibilities of illuminated intimate corners to sit on a warm summer's evening, enjoying the company of friends and making the most of those plants whose heady fragrances often seem so much more powerful after dark, like honeysuckle, night-scented stocks and night-scented tobacco plants (so much more intoxicating than the varieties bred for daytime enjoyment). Use your imagination to pick out interesting features, create pools of light and darkness, and cast dramatic shadows.

Time to enjoy

Garden lighting is just as effective whether you like throwing parties or simply enjoying the quiet companionship of friends in pleasant surroundings. During the day you are likely to be tempted to work and improve the garden, but the evening gives you the opportunity to sit back, relax and enjoy the fruits of your patient labours.

Lighting effects are not just confined to the summer months. For instance, a spotlight on a striking plant in winter, perhaps the pale ghost-like bark of a silver birch or the spiky purple leaves of a coloured New Zealand flax (*Phormium spp.*) rising from a layer of pure white snow, will create an arresting view from the warmth of the house no matter how uninviting the weather.

Easy for anyone

Safety is, of course, a major consideration when using electricity out of doors. In fact, many systems operate on a low voltage from a transformer in the home, so the outdoor cables are perfectly safe. If you live in a very sunny area, you can buy solar-powered garden lights that are completely independent of your mains supply. Even some of the mains lights, which are generally the most powerful and useful, are relatively easy to instal and safe to use as long as you take a few sensible precautions.

If you want lights in permanent positions, such as decorative lanterns by the drive, or porch lights, you will need a qualified electrician to instal them. It is worth having some outside sockets put in at the same time so that you can use them for power tools such as the mower.

Good garden lamps, even when clearly in view, highlight plants and other notable garden features such as the raised circular patio and the impressive stone blocks embedded with plants (right).

The feathery fronds of fennel (below) are lit up by a single, dedicated lamp, showing how imagination, and a willingness to experiment, can show you aspects of your garden which may previously have been hidden from view.

Hozelock Ltd.

Peter McHoy

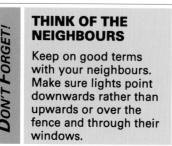

DON'T FORGET!

THINK OF THE NEIGHBOURS

Keep on good terms with your neighbours. Make sure lights point downwards rather than upwards or over the fence and through their windows.

Peterr McHoy

If you have a number of power points in various parts of the garden you will be able to move your lights around with ease, always being sure to use the special waterproof sockets. Run the cable in a conduit buried at least 45cm/18in below the ground and cover it with protective tiles. This reduces the risk of tripping over trailing wires as well as the risk of electrocution.

Safety first

Waterproof connectors must *always* be used outdoors and are readily available from water garden suppliers, garden centres and electrical shops. With any kind of mains outdoor light, always use a circuit-breaker, which will protect you if the wires are accidentally cut.

Low-voltage lights can be used with complete confidence and installed without the help of a qualified electrician, which makes them a much cheaper option. The small transformer that comes with them is simply plugged into a mains socket indoors or in a garage, and only the low-voltage cable is taken outdoors. The instructions will be simple to follow and the lights can usually be installed in less than an hour.

Remember, though, that trailing cables in the garden can still be a hazard. Make sure they are tucked out of harm's way.

If you simply want a carnival or party atmosphere for a special occasion, electric lights can be dispensed with. Candles, lamps and flares create all the atmosphere and mood you need. As these are purely temporary, they lack many of the advantages of a

A lantern can be useful to illuminate dark areas of the garden, even in daylight. This lantern (above) gives a warmth and security to its surrounding foliage. It is important to choose a colour of glass to suit your own needs. Some gardens benefit from stronger orange glows, some from whiter tones.

An array of 'novelty' lamps, such as these fanciful toadstools (right), are now available. Chosen wisely, they can add interest to your garden. But plan your lighting with care before you invest and be sure you have space to lay the wires without disturbing your plants.

Harry Smith Collection

permanent lighting system but you can have the best of both worlds by installing electric garden lighting for its year-round appeal, and supplementing it with flares and candles to create the right mood for a summer barbecue.

Lighting your garden does not necessarily have to be prohibitively expensive. One or two well chosen lights can be just as effective as dozens dotted around the garden, which will probably create a distracting collection of highlights.

Using light creatively

To make the most of creative garden lighting, you need to choose the right kind of light for the right position. For a festive theme, strings of coloured lights, cascading in loops from a trellis or wall, or threading their way through the branches of a tree, may be all that is required, especially if supplemented with candles and flares.

Many low-voltage systems are intended to cast a beam of light over a limited area: 'mushroom' types on thin stalks are intended to cast a beam of light down on to low bedding or perhaps carpeting ground cover plants like heathers, while pencil-shaped ones are for illuminating the way, perhaps at the edge of a path, and casting a little general light on to the surrounding flowers. These are practi-

cal and pretty, but in some gardens they may look too conspicuous during the day.

The most effective lights of all are spotlights that can be hidden behind shrubs or bushy plants. You do not see them during the day, and after dark they cast their beams to create startlingly beautiful effects. Most widely available garden spotlights have a spike that can be driven into the ground. Usually, they have swivel heads that can be repositioned to accommodate growing plants or cope with the changing seasons.

Choosing the angle

By turning the beam around, or altering its angle, you can highlight different plants as they come into flower, or pick out different 'architectural' shapes (like a contorted willow or a shapely *Fatsia japonica*) in the winter garden.

Another vital consideration is your choice of plants to highlight. Surprisingly, plants that may look terrific during the day can be disappointing in artificial light. A white flower will often stand out, though reds and blues can look muted and disappointing. Summer bedding is not always so striking by night either, so you need to experiment until you find groupings of plants that really do work when lit up.

Taking shape

Foliage plants, including those with variegated leaves, can be disappointing, but gold foliage or gold variegation can be striking. *Shape* is more important than colour after dark. A plain green hosta with big bold leaves like *H. sieboldiana* 'Elegans' can be more imposing than a prettily variegated one which you may prefer by day. Other border plants worth turning the spotlight on include bear's breeches *(Acanthus spinosus)*, *Crambe cordifolia* with its massive sprays of gypsophila-like white flowers on stems 1.8m/6ft or more

Harry Smith Collection

A garden light can fit snugly among border plants and foliage (above). The elegant statue lamp (right) is intended to be part of the garden sculpture, adding to its effect.

Patio lights are essential for outdoor dining (below) or simply reclining on a summer evening on the patio. They are available in a wide range of types and styles.

Harry Smith Collection

Peter McHoy

high, and red hot pokers (kniphofias). Some of the big grasses such as pampas grass look good in autumn.

If you have a herb garden, angelica and fennel are ideal subjects, and both of these can be grown in borders and in gravel too.

Bold shrubs or those with a strong outline like the false castor oil plant *(Fatsia japonica)*, phormiums, with their big sword-like leaves, hardy yuccas and the palm-like *Cordyline australis,* in areas where it is hardy, all look good bathed in light and also cast interesting shadows.

Lighting trees

Trees are often too large to illuminate effectively in a small garden, especially where stray light may annoy neighbours, but a small specimen tree like a corkscrew hazel or contorted willow will make a fine feature in winter.

Evergreen plants like the Australian gums (eucalyptus) show up well at any time of the year. It is not always necessary to illuminate the whole tree – the silvery-white trunk of a birch, perhaps set against a dark hedge, can create a splendidly dramatic effect.

Spotlights can be especially effective picking out an ornament or statue. A simple bust on a plinth, perhaps set in an alcove or backed by a brick wall, will look wonderful framed by plants like ivy and picked out in a spotlight.

Try moving a light around before you fix it, shining it from low and high angles, from first one side and then the other – all will affect the amount of detail revealed, and the effect of the moving shadows is a marvellous lesson in the use of lights.

BY THE LIGHT OF THE SUN

Solar lights for the evening garden may sound improbable, but they may be just what you want if wires and transformers do not appeal and a soft, diffused light is what you are looking for, though do not expect the same effect as a mains spotlight. They are fine for summer evenings, when the stored energy is released as light, but they clearly have limitations for winter use in climates that are far from sunny.

A solar-powered unit (left) uses state-of-the-art equipment. Another boon is that it is entirely free of the mains system, which gives added flexibility and saves time in the installation. But take good advice from a reliable dealer or experienced friends to ensure that you have the right amount of sunlight needed to operate this equipment. Some gardens may receive enough natural light for only a few weeks every year. Many people do find solar units a very shrewd investment.

Photos Horticultural

PARTY LIGHTS AND FLARES

Party lights, which can be bought from garden centres and large DIY stores, are inexpensive, easy to put up, and do not need permanent wiring. Just plug them indoors and run the lead out through a window for the occasion. Instructions will come with the lights, which you can also use around the porch or a window for Christmas. Small oil-filled lamps, usually described as patio lamps, are another option, and these are useful for their flickering, atmospheric light.

Candles also contribute to the party atmosphere on a summer's evening, and they will help to illuminate a table. Some are perfumed, and may contain a fragrance to keep insects away. You may find this useful if you do not find the night-flying moths and insects welcome visitors.

Flares on a stick or cane that you simply push into the ground produce more light, and children find them fun. Although the burning time depends on the make and type, most will burn for several hours.

BRIGHT IDEAS

Index

*P*hotographic *C*redits

ANDREW LAWSON 7, *9*, *13*, *15*, *17*, *29*, *33*, *47*, *64*, *87*
BASCO BARON, ROCHDALE *74*; BULLDOG GARDEN BUILDINGS *68*
COLLECTIONS *15*, *28*, *34*, *77*; DAVID SQUIRE *16*, *17*, *71*, *83*
DEREK GOULD *6*, *10*, *24*, *38*, *39*, *41*, *46*, *63*, *73*, *86*, *89*
DON WILDRIDGE *12*, *37*; ELIZABETH WHITING *55*, *57*, *58*
ERIC CRICHTON *11*, *21*, *25*, *31*, *48*, *59*, *69*, *75*, *76*, *79*, *85*, *87*, *89*
GARDEN PICTURE LIBRARY 8, *16*, 18, 20, *26*, *29*, *32*, *43*, *56*, *66*, *70*, *72*, *82*; GILLIAN BECKETT *88*
HARRY SMITH COLLECTION *19*, *23*, *24*, *26*, *35*, *37*, *42*, *43*, *44*, *52*, *56*, *57*, *58*, *59*, *71*, *76*, *77*, *78*, *80*, *84*, *91*, *92*
LIFE FILE *81*, *84*; MARSHALL CAVENDISH *31*, *36*, *81*
NATURE PHOTOGRAPHS *14*
NEIL HOLMES 8, *9*, *40*, *41*, *45*, *47*
NHPA *19*, *20*, *21*
P.J. BRIDGEMAN & CO LTD, ENFIELD, *68*
PAT BRINDLEY *13*, *15*, *33*, *36*, *40*, *46*, *49*, *51*
PETER McHOY 8, *10*, *19*, *36*, *44*, *54*, *68*, *90*, *91*, *92*
PHOTOS HORTICULTURAL *10*, *11*, *14*, *27*, *28*, *30*, *33*, *34*, *38*, *40*, *42*, *49*, *50*, *51*, *52*, *53*, *58*, *62*, *63*, *67*, *69*, *78*, *87*, *88*, *93*
S & O MATHEWS *30*, *62*, *64*, *65*, *74*, *78*
TANIA MIDGLEY *13*, *25*, *35*, *45*